HE WILL COME TO US LIKE THE RAIN

downpour

James MacDonald

with message-music CD by
Harvest Songs

learning activities and leader guide by
Barb Peil & Claude King

LifeWay Press®
Nashville, Tennessee

Published by LifeWay Press® • © 2006 James MacDonald • Reprinted 2017

ISBN 978-1-4158-2925-7 • Item 001303830

Dewey decimal classification: 248.84
Subject headings: CHRISTIAN LIFE \ DISCIPLESHIP

To order additional copies of this resource, write to LifeWay Resources Customer Service; One LifeWay Plaza; Nashville, TN 37234-0113; fax 615-251-5933; phone toll free 800-458-2772; email orderentry@lifeway.com; order online at LifeWay.com; or visit the LifeWay Christian Store serving you.

Printed in the United States of America

Groups Ministry Publishing • LifeWay Resources
One LifeWay Plaza • Nashville, TN 37234-0152

contents

9/17

9/24

10/1

10/8

10/22

10/29

11/5

11/12

11-26

12-3 1-7

1-14

12-13 Christmas lunch

1-21- MLK DAY

1-28 - New Series

the author

James MacDonald has committed his life to the unapologetic proclamation of God's Word. He is the founder and senior pastor of Harvest Bible Chapel, one of the fastest-growing churches in the Chicago area, reaching more than 13,000 lives each weekend. Heard on the "Walk in the Word" radio and television broadcasts, his practical teaching is also accessed by thousands online. Through James's leadership and by God's grace, Harvest Bible Fellowship, the church-planting ministry he founded in 2002, has planted more than one hundred churches across North America and around the world.

Born in London, Ontario, Canada, James received his master's degree from Trinity Evangelical Divinity School in Deerfield, Illinois, and his doctorate from Phoenix Seminary. He and his wife, Kathy, have three adult children and reside in Chicago. For more information about James and these ministries, visit harvestbible.org or walkintheword.org.

Other Books by James MacDonald

Act like Men (Moody, 2014)
Always True: God's Promises When Life Is Hard Bible study (LifeWay, 2011)
Always True: God's Five Promises When Life Is Hard (Moody, 2011)
Authentic: Developing the Disciplines of a Sincere Faith Bible study (LifeWay, 2013)
Authentic: Developing the Disciplines of a Sincere Faith (Moody, 2013)
Come Home: A Call Back to Faith Bible study (LifeWay, 2014)
Come Home: A Call Back to Faith (Moody, 2013)
Downpour: He Will Come to Us like the Rain (B&H, 2006)
God Wrote a Book (Crossway, 2002)
Gripped by the Greatness of God (Moody, 2005)
Have the Funeral small-group study (LifeWay, 2011)
Lord, Change Me (Moody, 2012)
Lord, Change My Attitude Before It's Too Late Bible study (LifeWay, 2008)
Lord, Change My Attitude … Before It's Too Late (Moody, 2001)
Seven Words to Change Your Family (Moody, 2002)
Ten Choices: A Proven Plan to Change Your Life Forever (Thomas Nelson, 2008)
Think Differently Bible study (LifeWay, 2016)
Vertical Church (David C Cook, 2012)
Vertical Church Bible study (LifeWay, 2012)
When Life Is Hard Bible study (LifeWay, 2010)
When Life Is Hard (Moody, 2010)

Learning Activities and Leader Guide

Barb Peil is the communications director for James MacDonald's radio ministry, Walk in the Word, and **Claude King** is a discipleship specialist at LifeWay Christian Resources.

introduction

Welcome to *Downpour*. Of all the sermons I've preached over the years, the themes in this study are the core of my life message. I'm praying that you will experience a downpour of God's grace as you participate in this study with other believers. Before we get into the message, allow me to give you an overview of the process.

This Bible study book may be a little different from books you have read before. I not only want you to receive the message, but I also want you to respond to the message. To do that, I've provided a variety of activities to guide you along the way. Each week you will listen to a DVD message. Then during the following week, you will study five daily lessons to help you understand and apply the truths to your life. A small group of other believers will help you process what you hear and learn. My prayer is that God will guide you by His Spirit to experience a downpour of His blessings.

When you travel on a highway, you see road signs alerting you to upcoming conditions that may require caution or call for certain actions. Some give you rules for the road to provide the safest and best experience. Following are some road signs for our study.

① **When you see a colored, circled number, I'm inviting you to complete an activity or respond to a question. These activities will help you develop your understanding of the text and apply the truths to your life.**

When you look at the man on the cover of this book, you see someone who has symbolically removed the barriers that keep him from experiencing God's downpour. I'll use this symbol to point you to God in prayer. Don't omit these prayer activities or rush through them. They may be the most important things you do in this study. After all, God is the One we are seeking. These prayer activities give you opportunities to connect with Him. Enjoy your times with Him.

◎ **When you see this CD symbol, it alerts you to an activity based on the Message-Music CD at the back of the book. Listen to the *Downpour* revival songs and meditate on the lyrics of each song. Allow God to speak to your mind and your heart as you listen.**

A big umbrella like the one below is what I call a reader stopper. It follows an assignment that takes some time. When you see this umbrella, STOP. Ask yourself, *Did I complete the activity just assigned?* If not, do so before continuing your work.

✝ When you see a small umbrella, you will know you've reached the end of the day or the end of the article. Take a break after each day's lesson. Spread the study over the week to allow time to assimilate the message into your life. Don't rush through the study at the last minute before your small-group session. Doing so will short-circuit your learning. Soak in the message one day at a time.

Pictures of Personal Revival

Each week I will guide you to study a personal revival either from Scripture or from more recent history. These illustrations from the lives of others should increase your faith to believe God for personal revival in your life. Some will give you examples of how to respond to the Lord. Others may prompt and guide you to pray more specifically. They may also help you identify genuine revival when God begins to pour it on and around your life.

Activate

As you study each of the five major messages in *Downpour*, your head may be full of information, but I want to help you move the focus from your head to your heart. To do so, I will give you an "Activate" assignment. This step will give you something to think about, something to do, or a fresh way to make God's truth your own. You will see real change in your life only as you personalize the truth by your actions.

Elevate

Need a place to begin with God? Let these written prayers start your conversation with Him and then keep it going on your own. Wait in silence when the words don't come. Pray with expectation, believing that God hears you and will respond.

Replicate

The Christian life was never meant to be lived solo. God designed His people to interact and help one another grow. Make a specific commitment to share with at least one other person what you are learning about personal revival. Don't neglect this critical step! You'll be surprised at the results.

Small Group

If you are preparing to study this book alone, I encourage you to find at least one other person or a small group to join you on the journey. We need one another as followers of Christ. A group can encourage you to press on to know and serve the Lord.

Let's begin the journey with prayer. Ask God to open your ears to hear and your eyes to see all He has in store for your life in the coming weeks. Give Him permission to mold and shape your life in a way that will bring Him pleasure and glory.

week 1

we need a downpour

week 1

we need a downpour

key verse to memorize

*"Come, let us return to the Lord; for he has torn us, that he
may heal us; he has struck us down, and he will bind us up."*
Hosea 6:1

For session 1 plans, turn to page 169 in the leader guide.

getting acquainted with your small group
Introduce yourself and explain why you have chosen to participate in a study
of *Downpour*. Answer one of the following:
1. What are your personal reasons for joining this small group? OR
2. What do you hope to receive from this study?

dvd session 1 message notes (56 minutes)
Scripture focus: Hosea 6:1-3

I. The _invitation_ to revival
   A. Let's turn to the _LORD_ (v. 1). *Col 2:6 So walk in Him*
   "Return" (Hos. 5:4; 7:10; 11:5; 14:4)
   1. Recognition – *problems*
   2. Repent – *change our minds - I was wrong*
   3. Returning – *danger - I have to get it together*
   B. Let's _KNOW_ *come as you are* the Lord (v. 3). *internal seeking*
   1. Facts about the Lord – *FACTS*
   2. Heart understanding of the facts *Ex 5:2*
   3. Experience with God *Acts 17:28* *Rom 13:11*
   4. Blessings from God *James 1:17*
II. The _Pathway_ to revival
   A. Through _Pain_ to purpose (v. 1). *Job 5:17-18*
   B. Through _DEATH_ to life (vv. 1-2).
III. The _DEFINITION EXPERIENCE_ of revival
   A. It's _Available_ (v. 3). *as certain as dawn*
   B. It's _abundant_ (v. 3).

🔘 Message music: see the "Downpour" lyrics on page 10.

8

1. God on the Throne
2. Sin in mirror - a picture of brokenness
3. Self in the dirt - a picture of repentance
4. Christ on the cross - a picture of grace
5. Spirit in control - a picture of power

snapshot summary

God wants to revive our relationship with Him. Revival is renewed interest after a period of indifference or decline. He wants to wake us up, to refresh our faith, to fire us up again.

my goals for you

I want you to understand what revival is and how God accomplishes that work in your life, and I want you to show your openness to remove the barriers that could limit your experience of God's downpour.

responding to the message

1. Review by answering the following questions:
   a. What is revival?
   b. What are the three steps in turning back to the Lord?
   c. Why do we sometimes need a fresh crisis to call us back to the Lord?
   d. What does Hosea mean by pressing on to know the Lord?
   e. What is God's typical pathway to revival?
   f. What evidence in our lives, church, community, or nation indicates that we need revival?
2. Have you ever had a wake-up call that caused you think more seriously about eternal things? Is so, what happened and how did you respond?
3. Invite volunteers to pray sentence prayers for God to reveal Himself and revive you and your church.

small-group agreements

As a group, discuss and agree to the following commitments. Then join hands and pray for God's special work in your group and your church during the coming weeks.
- I will privately spend time completing the daily study and learning activities in my *Downpour* Bible study book.
- I will make every effort to attend the weekly sessions.
- I will pray regularly for my fellow group members.
- I will receive the direction and challenge given in the DVD message and in my small-group activities with the desire to apply them to my life.
- I will participate openly and honestly in our group discussions.
- I will keep confidential any personal matters shared by others in the group.
- I will pray at least weekly for revival in our church.

Message-notes blanks: invitation, Lord, know, pathway, pain, death, experience, available, abundant

downpour

here where self and sin and sadness / have displaced the oil of gladness
here in barren desert madness, / weary and dry
cannot run or walk, I'm crawling, / but through shame I hear You calling
clouds of mercy, raindrops falling / downpour, I need a downpour

come, come like the rain,
wash every stain, fall upon me Jesus
river of God, flooding with joy,
rise up in me, Jesus

into my heart's desolation / flows the water of salvation
fill this lowly wasteland with the / shower from above
only You can quench my thirsting, / fill until my heart is bursting
Jesus ever be the first thing / downpour, I need a downpour

*"He will come to us as the showers,
as the spring rains that water the earth."*
Hosea 6:3

Slowly read the lyrics above and meditate on the meaning of this song. Use the following questions to reflect on your own need for and desire for a downpour.

1. Have self, sin, and sadness robbed you of joy and gladness?
2. Spiritually, do you feel barren, weary, and dry or parched?
3. Are you spiritually crippled by sin or shame?
4. How would you describe your personal desire for God's mercy drops, raindrops, downpour?

Use the last two paragraphs of the song as a prayer to Jesus. Listen to the song on your Message-Music CD (track 1) at the back of this book and let this become your prayer for the coming weeks. Pray for a personal downpour in your life and in the lives of others in your group and in your church.

day 1 | We Need a Downpour

There's something about a dry spell that gets people talking. I've been hearing it from almost everyone: "Man, this has been a dry summer." Yep, there's no denying it, the lack of rain is a big deal. Lawns are dead, fruit stands are deserted, and farmers are defeated. This past summer will go down in the record books as a parched and desolate season, but was it the driest summer we've ever had? Not even close.

If your grandparents are around, they could probably tell you about a drought in the 1930s when it didn't rain for nine years. In the breadbasket of the country, our richest farmlands were turned into a dust bowl. In 1934, 34 states experienced severe droughts. On April 14, 1935, a day known as Black Sunday, the wind whipped across the parched farmland and blew up the dust into an enormous black blizzard that whisked away countless acres of topsoil. That's what a drought is like, and most of us have never experienced a real one—not in our countryside, at least. But sadly, too often we experience a drought in our spirits.

The Bible teaches in Isaiah 58:11 and in many other places that the human heart is like a garden. Your heart is the immaterial part of you that can know God; it's the part that will live forever. If you weed and water and tend your heart as Scripture instructs, you'll experience a bumper crop of God's grace in your life. Conversely, if you fail to garden your heart, first it will become overgrown with weeds, then it will become lifeless and dry, and eventually it will disappear in a spiritual dust storm. Second Corinthians 4 twice exhorts us not to lose heart because if we do, we've lost everything. No wonder the wisest man who ever lived exhorted, "Guard your heart!" (Prov. 4:23, NIV). You have to take care of your heart.

1 **If you and God examined the spiritual condition of the garden in your heart today, what would you find? Check one or write your own.**
   ❏ a. Moist, tender, flourishing
   ❏ b. Getting dry and needing rain
   ❏ c. Drought conditions, dusty, cracked, hard
   ❏ d. Other: _____

Like me, maybe you've experienced some parched days in your relationship with God. Maybe you've known the sadness of falling in exhaustion and watching through weary eyes as your heart for something or someone begins to shrivel. Maybe you've had seasons when time with God was nonexistent and weekend worship was Black Sunday for sure—not because of where the pastor or the people were in their hearts but because of where you were in yours. Now hear this: times of refreshing may come from the presence of the Lord (see Acts 3:20). The goal of this chapter is for you to begin to believe that.

You—yes, YOU—can have a fresh downpour of God's grace and mercy on your life. The hands that hold this book can feel a fresh surge of energy to labor for our King. The eyes that see these pages can gaze in renewed wonder and awe on the God who loves you. The heart that beats within your chest this moment can pulse with renewed joy given by God in response to choices you make and actions you take. Honest! God is not reluctant; He is ready and willing.

Read again this amazing assurance given by the prophet Hosea: "Come, let us return to the LORD; for he has torn us, that he may heal us; he has struck us down, and he will bind us up. After two days he will revive us; on the third day he will raise us up, that we may live before him. Let us know; let us press on to know the LORD; his going out is sure as the dawn; he will come to us as the showers, as the spring rains that water the earth" (Hos. 6:1-3).

> **Pause to pray and ask God to work in your life in the ways He knows you need Him so that your life will flourish with the joy of His presence and the fruitfulness He desires.**

What Do We Mean by Revival?

② **What do you think of when you read the word *revival?* Check one or write your own.**
- ❏ a. Tent meetings
- ❏ b. Crazy things happening like people barking and jumping around
- ❏ c. Masses of people getting saved
- ❏ d. Television evangelists
- ❏ e. Other: *renewal - coming back to God*

Sadly, when you say the word *revival* today, people think of all the circus chicanery and religious nonsense that accompany flesh-induced spiritual fervor. For that reason I must spend a moment explaining what I don't mean by revival.

Revival is not long lines of anxious sinners waiting for a turn at the microphone to reveal their most secret sinful something. That's not revival. Revival is not emotional extravagance where people are caught up in the moment and fall down, act bizarrely, unbiblically, and out of control. That's not revival.

③ **As you read the following section, underline the words, phrases, or sentences that help define what we mean by the word *revival.* I've underlined one for you.**

The Bible teaches clearly and repeatedly that God wants to revive our relationship with Him. <u>Revival is renewed interest after a period of indifference or decline.</u> He wants to wake us up, to refresh our faith—to fire us up again. The word *revive* is used many times in Scripture. Let's look at a few.
- "I am exceedingly afflicted;
  Revive me … according to Your word" (Ps. 119:107, NASB).
- "Turn away my eyes from looking at vanity,
  and revive me in Your ways" (Ps. 119:37, NASB).
- "Revive us, and we will call upon Your name" (Ps. 80:18, NASB).

Revival involves an increased hunger for and delight in God's Word after a difficult season of life (Ps. 119:107). Revival involves a disdain for sin and a renewed desire for obedience to God (Ps. 119:37). And revival brings increased commitment to and interest in personal prayer (Ps. 80:18).

Revival is getting back on the path, getting the goal in view again, and pursuing with new passion the One who can make your life more than you ever dreamed. Revival is God, gladly at the center of my life, experienced and enjoyed. I see God working. He's working in my life, and I'm loving it more and more. That's revival.

4 **Write a definition of *revival*, using your own words or a combination of words above.**

Revival is *awareness of God*

renewal

Described another way: revival is God's response to a people thirsty for Him.

5 **What are you thirsty for? What does your heart long for in your relationship with God? Check all that apply or write your own.**
- ☑ A deeper relationship with God
- ☑ More consistent growth in my inner life
- ☑ Patterns of sinful thoughts and behavior broken
- ☑ Forgiveness extended and received
- ☑ Deeper awareness of God's love for me
- ☑ Greater love for Christ
- ☑ To be used in others' lives and for God's greater kingdom
- ☑ My life to bear much fruit
- ❑ Other: _____

6 **What is the "umbrella" ☂ in your life that hinders or gets between you and the downpour of God's presence, power, and vitality?**

my own self

_____

Conclude today's lesson in prayer. Express to God your desire for personal revival. Give Him permission to begin His work in you. Use your own words or the ones below if you mean them.

God, my heart has grown dry. I have allowed some of the truth of Your Word to become fact-based, and my heart needs to be refreshed by Your Spirit. Bring a fresh move of revival into our church and into our lives. Give me faith and grace this week to move toward You for a personal reviving of my life in You. Forgive my callousness and indifference. Do a fresh work of Your Spirit in my life, I ask. Thank You for your grace and Your goodness that You promise to respond to my heart's cry with a downpour of blessing. Thank You that You are a God of a second chance. I seek You now with all my heart. Prepare my heart for what You have in store for me. In Jesus' name. Amen. ✝

| # Josiah's Personal Revival

Revival is renewed interest after a period of indifference or decline. It is God, gladly at the center of my life, experienced and enjoyed. One of the first barriers to revival we may face, however, is the pride that says with attitude, *What have I done?*

In Hosea 7:10 we read, "The pride of Israel testifies to his face; yet they do not return to the LORD their God, nor seek him." It's not easy to admit that my heart is parched and dry. It's not easy to confess that what I set off in search of has not delivered what it promised. It's hard to swallow my pride and say that what I really needed is back where I left it, waiting for my return. Today I want you to see an example of personal revival in Scripture when a king overcame his pride.

1 **Read about the picture of personal revival from the life of Josiah on the opposite page. As time permits, read one or more of the biblical accounts in 2 Kings 22:1–23:27 or 2 Chronicles 34–35.**

2 **How did Josiah respond when He heard God's Word read for the first time?**
  ❏ a. He was filled with joy because he was hearing God's Word for His people.
  ❏ b. He was terrified. He realized he and those before him had sinned greatly against the Lord and stood in danger of God's judgment.

3 **How did God respond to Josiah's humility and repentance?**
  ❏ a. He revived His people and spared that generation from experiencing the consequences of their sin.
  ❏ b. He ignored Josiah's appeal for mercy and brought about the destruction He had promised in His Word.

Close today's study in prayer. Ask God to reveal pride or any other sin that may be a barrier to personal revival. Then throw away that "umbrella" and seek the Lord. ☂

From the Life of Josiah: We Need a Downpour

2 KINGS 22:1–23:27; 2 CHRONICLES 34–35; DEUTERONOMY 28:15

The storm clouds had never looked darker over Judah than they did in 640 B.C. Unchecked evil reigned, from the king's palace down to the streets. God's people had not only forgotten Him; now they provoked His anger with their wickedness. God's holy patience had run out. "Enough," He sighed and started the countdown to judgment.

But to everyone's surprise, out from that dark heritage walked the boy-king Josiah, who "did what was right in the eyes of the LORD" (2 Kings 22:2). Standing in the gap between God's holiness and his people's wickedness, young Josiah launched a lifelong crusade to take care of God's business in Judah. His mission was clear: we're turning back to God.

Then an amazing thing happened. As Josiah's team rebuilt God's temple, in ruins after generations of neglect, they found God's Book buried in obscurity. At age 26 Josiah read God's Word for the first time, and it took him to his knees.

He hadn't known that God had written down His instructions. He hadn't heard the promises of warning and blessing based on obedience. And now his heart was exposed to God's Word for the first time, and it convicted him to the core.

Josiah realized they were sitting on a time bomb. "Great is the wrath of the LORD that is kindled against us, because our fathers have not obeyed the words of this book" (2 Kings 22:13). The clock had been ticking all the time God's Word had been buried, and judgment was closer than they had realized.

So as a man before God and a king before his nation, Josiah invited God's Word to change their thinking.

- He recognized that some things had to go. *We're going to live differently.*
- He repented of how his nation had walked away from God. *We've been wrong, and we're turning around.*
- He and his people returned to the Lord. *We're leaving this sin behind us. We want what God has for us.*

His mission was again clear: revive us, Lord. We need a downpour!

What happened next changed history. God saw the tenderness and humility of Josiah's heart and had compassion on him and his generation. In His holiness God could not overlook the evil that had been done, but He held back the clock so that this repentant generation would not experience the consequences.

Revival begins here: with a profound awareness of God's absolute holiness, our absolute sinfulness, and our complete inability to bridge the divide that separates us. Revival always begins with God reaching down to us—not in a trickle of blessing but in a deluge of Himself that covers our past and welcomes us to begin again. ✝

Your Spiritual Timeline

Activate

When you go to a doctor for the first time, the doctor or a nurse takes time to ask you lots of questions about your medical history. This information will help the doctor understand you and better diagnose your health or illness. Today I want to check out your spiritual history for similar reasons. Where have you been with the Lord? Where are you now? Where are you headed?

As you begin, pause to pray and ask the Lord to bring to your memory the experiences that make up your spiritual history.

① Draw a spiritual timeline in the space on the opposite page.
Check the instructions below as you complete them.
- ❏ Begin by drawing a horizontal line across the width of the paper. For more space draw two or more lines and split your timeline in pieces or turn the page to a landscape format.
- ❏ Label the left point with your birth date and draw a vertical line at every five-year increment to the present. Label those markers with the year.
- ❏ Draw a bold dot on your timeline for every significant event in your life (salvation, graduations, wedding dates, births/deaths of loved ones, career milestones, relocations, etc.). Label them with short descriptions.
- ❏ Draw another bold dot above or below the line describing the mountaintops or valleys in your spiritual life and write above it what your relationship with God was like during that time. When did God show up? When did you not see His hand? When was your relationship satisfying or stale?
- ❏ Write somewhere on the page, "Lord, bring a downpour to my life." Describe in as many words as it takes what you would like God to do in your life. Place an X on the timeline, marking today. Write above it, "Lord, start here."

Elevate

Slowly pray through the following prayer. Make it your own.

Lord, I'm choosing today as my crisis. I am turning around. I am pressing on to know You. Take me to a new level of belonging to You. Reign over me as I've never known before.

Lord, nothing is off-limits to You. Go anywhere in my life and say anything to me. No place of sinfulness, no place of defeat or selfishness or self-indulgence is hidden from You. All that I am and have, it's Yours.

I'm weary of being dry and passionless. See the true condition of my heart. Thank You for the assurances of Your grace as I am now responding to Your awesome invitation. Immerse me in a mighty work of Your Spirit that eclipses everything I've experienced to date. Start today, Lord. I need a downpour. ✝

downpour

day 4 | Your New Life in Christ

Don't Get the Cart Before the Horse

Don't attempt to be *revived* if you have never been "vived" in the first place. Second Corinthians 5:17 says that if any of us "is in Christ, he is a new creation; the old has gone, the new has come!" (NIV) Have you found that new life in Christ? Have you had a conversion experience? Have you been "vived"? Don't get the cart before the horse. There is no point in pursuing re-vival if you have never been "vived."

1 Can you tell a story like this?

There was a time in my life when I was going the wrong way, and the Lord reached out and brought me to the cross. By faith I experienced the forgiveness of sin that Jesus died and rose again to provide. At that time my eyes were opened, my heart was gripped, my life was captured by the grace of God, and I have never been the same since.

❏ Yes   ❏ No

If your answer is yes because you have new life in Christ, jump down to "Replicate" below. If you have never experienced this new life in Jesus Christ, keep reading. The story above is the real-life testimony for every person who has been given life in Christ. You can be come to new life here in this moment if you pray this prayer to God from your heart:"

Lord, I know that I am a sinner and that on my own I am not prepared to meet God. I believe that Jesus died to pay the penalty for my sin. I believe that He rose from the dead. Right now in this moment I turn from my sin, and I embrace Jesus Christ by faith. Come into my life and forgive my sins. Change me. Make me the man (or woman) You want me to be. I give my life to You today. I pray in Jesus' name. Amen.

2 If you prayed this prayer because you were ready to repent and turn to Christ for salvation and life, tell somebody in your family and in your small group. Let them rejoice with you in this decision.

Replicate: Remembering the Joy of Your Salvation

We're focusing in this study on personal revival—a bringing back to life after indifference or decline. No matter how long it's been since you've come to Jesus as your Savior, think back to the joy of your salvation.

3 Want to really fire up your passion for God? Prepare to share with your small group a brief testimony of how you came to Christ for salvation. Though you may or may not have a dramatic testimony, remember that every transformed life is a miracle. Keep your time focused on your point of crisis as the prompting for your initial decision to trust Christ.

Spend time in prayer thanking God for His great salvation. ↑

downpour

day 5 | Personal Revival in the First Great Awakening

1 **Read on page 20 about the picture of personal revival from the First Great Awakening. Pay attention to the ways God used pain, death, and crisis to revive the hearts of people and bring others to faith in Christ.**

2 **How would you describe the "dullness of religion" in our day? Write words, phrases, or a sentence or two.**

_____

_____

_____

3 **Which of the following happenings do you think contributed most to the stirring of hearts to turn to the Lord? Check one.**
- ❏ a. The death of the two young people in a nearby village
- ❏ b. The preaching of God's Word on justification by faith
- ❏ c. The dramatic conversion of the woman who was "one of the greatest company keepers" (probably a prostitute)

Why? _____

_____

Close this week's study in prayer.
- Pray that God will use every opportunity to bring about a time of crisis to turn your heart and the hearts of God's people back to Him.
- Pray that your life will be a powerful testimony of the transformation Christ can produce in a life through salvation.
- Pray that God will pour down on your town the kind of mercy and grace He poured out on Northampton.
- Pray for the members of your small group as you prepare yourselves to hear and respond to God and His Word over the coming weeks. ↑

Jonathan Edwards and the First Great Awakening (1734)

If you asked people living in the early 1730s in the original 13 American colonies to direct you to a church on fire for God, they would have shrugged their shoulders and shaken their heads. People's hearts were far from God.

Jonathan Edwards, a pastor in Northampton, Massachusetts, described it as a "degenerate time" marked by a "dullness of religion." The young people were addicted to night walking, tavern drinking, lewd practices among the sexes the greater part of the night. "Family government did too much fail in the town." For years the town had been sharply divided between two feuding parties. Edwards fervently prayed for individuals to turn back to God.

In a nearby village, 2 young people suddenly died in the spring of 1734. The town was jarred into thinking about their eternal destinies. People began to seek God. That fall Edwards preached on justification by faith alone, and 6 persons received Christ. One of them was a young woman who was "one of the greatest company keepers in the whole town." Her life was so radically changed that everyone could tell it was a work of God's grace. Over the next six months 300 people were "hopefully converted" in this town of 1,100.[1] Edwards said:

God seemed to have gone out of His usual way in the quickness of His work, and the swift progress His Spirit has made in His operation on the hearts of many. ... There was scarcely a single person in the town, either old or young, that was left unconcerned about the great things of the eternal world. ... The town seemed to be full of the presence of God: it never was so full of love, nor so full of joy. ... Our public assemblies were then beautiful; the congregation was alive in God's service. ... Our public praises were then greatly enlivened.[2]

It was this revival, and Edwards's reporting of it, that provoked people on both sides of the Atlantic to seek God for a downpour of mercy in their lives. They were not disappointed. Under the leadership of men like Jonathan Edwards, George Whitefield, and John Wesley, the church grew very rapidly in New England between 1740 and 1742, with more than 300,000 new and revived Christians turning to the Lord in faith and repentance. One historian called this time "The most glorious and extensive revival our country has ever known." ↑

1. Henry Blackaby and Claude King, *Fresh Encounter* (Nashville: LifeWay Press, 1996), 42.
2. Adapted from Jonathan Edwards, "Narrative of Surprising Conversions," in *The Works of President Edwards* (New York: Leavitt & Allen, 1857), 231–72, as quoted by Blackaby and King, 42.

downpour

God on the throne: a picture of holiness

PART 1

God on the throne: a picture of holiness

PART 1

key verse to memorize

*"Holy, holy, holy is the Lord of hosts;
the whole earth is full of his glory!"*

Isaiah 6:3

For session 2 plans, turn to page 169 in the leader guide.

discussion guide on week 1: we need a downpour

1. Share your desire for personal revival and what you've learned in the first week. The effort to express your vision for personal revival has great benefit—to you and to others!
2. Volunteers, share a brief testimony of how you came to Christ for salvation (activity 3, p. 18).
3. Volunteers, share your responses to activities 1, 2, and 5 (day 1, pp. 11–13).
4. How would you define *revival*? (activity 4, p. 13)
5. How did Josiah respond when he heard God's Word read? How did God respond to that repentant generation?
6. Review Hosea 6:1-3. How would you describe the events of the First Great Awakening as an example of the fulfillment of God's promises in Hosea?
7. Volunteers, share some of the high points on your spiritual timeline. Have you ever experienced personal revival? If so, describe your experience.

dvd session 2 message notes (27 minutes)

Scripture focus: Isaiah 6:1-4

　　Throne room 1—Isaiah's vision
1. Holiness describes _Seperation different_ (v. 1; Ezek. 1:1,3,26-28).
　　Throne room 2—Ezekiel's vision (Ezek. 1)
2. Holiness demands _Caution_ (v. 2; Rev. 20:11).
　　Throne room 3—John's view of the Great White Throne (Rev. 20:11-12)

Testimony: Josh's story from rock star to Christian musician

　　　　　　　　Luke 23:30

snapshot summary

A right view of God's holiness is the beginning place for personal revival. God is more righteous and pure, more piercing and powerful, more strong and impenetrable than anything we can imagine. He's different, separate, other, holy.

my goals for you

I want you to understand the seriousness of responding properly to God because of His holiness, and I want you to approach Him with caution.

responding to the message

1. Review by answering the following questions:
   a. Why is a clear view or understanding of God important for us?
   b. How would you define *holiness?*
   c. How did men and angels respond to the vision of God's holiness?
   d. If necessary, read again the three throne-room scenes in Isaiah 6, Ezekiel 1, and Revelation 20. What do we learn about God and His throne room from Isaiah, Ezekiel, and John?
2. If you encountered God in His holiness today, what would be an appropriate response?
3. Spend time in prayer. Praise God for His holiness and purity. Describe to Him your awe and reverent fear. Pray for His help in responding correctly to His holiness.

preview statements for this week's study

- The downpour begins with an exalted view of God.
- God is more righteous and pure, more piercing and powerful, more strong and impenetrable than anything we can imagine.
- He is holy. He is separate. He is completely unlike us.
- When God is humanized and man is deified, holiness is lost.
- Preferring the comfort of His nearness, we have lost the reality of God's transcendent holiness.
- "Sow for yourselves righteousness; reap steadfast love; break up your fallow ground, for it is the time to seek the Lord, that he may come and rain righteousness upon you" (Hos. 10:12).

Message-notes blanks: separation, caution

| # Holiness Describes Separation

There can be no personal revival without a right view of God. If you want *more of God* in your life, begin with "more accurate."

1 **What comes to your mind when you think about God? What do you picture when you consider deity? Not what do you think He looks like, but how do you envision God's capacities and interests? What do you believe matters to Him, and where do you conclude His great interests and passions reside? Write words or phrases that immediately come to mind as you think about the essential nature of God and His work.**

all knowing   all loving
all seeing   holy
all powerful

A. W. Tozer rightly observed that what you think about God is the most important thing about you. It's true whether or not you realize it: your entire life revolves around your view of God. Your personal spiritual revival is waiting. The downpour begins with an exalted view of God.

The Bible repeatedly reveals that the God of the universe resides in a throne room; He is there right now. Through the centuries God in His grace has allowed certain messengers to visit His throne room. Over the course of the next two weeks, we are going to see God's throne room afresh through their eyes.

Before we begin, let's get a definition on the table that will serve us well on our tour. The single word that summarizes God, His presence, and His throne room—all things that relate to God—is the word *holiness*.

What Exactly Is Holiness?

The Hebrew term is *qodesh;* the Greek is *hagios*. Both mean *to be set apart.* When we say "holiness," we mean God is not like us at all, not in any way. He's different. We would say "awesome" or "unbelievable" or "unfathomable." That's holiness. God is more righteous and pure, more piercing and powerful, more strong and impenetrable than anything we can imagine. We comprehend only fractionally, even infinitesimally, all that He is. He's so different—so other—so holy. Every time you hear the word *holy,* think separation; God is completely apart and entirely different from you and me.

2 **Check the words that best describe holiness. Check all that apply.**

❑ same	☑ set apart	❑ common
☑ different	☑ dedicated	❑ ordinary
☑ pure	❑ polluted	❑ corrupt
❑ clean	☑ righteous	☑ other

downpour

All of the previous words might contribute to our understanding of *holiness* except *corrupt, polluted, ordinary, common,* and *same.* If we're going to see revival in our lives, it has to start here: a right view of the infinitely exalted nature of God Himself. All revival flows from this fountain: a biblical view of God Himself. He is holy.

I Don't Want That!

At the core of our sinfulness is our desire to usurp God. Can you admit that? Because of our ancestry in the garden of Eden, we were born with the desire to gain the position that belongs to God and God alone. In Genesis 3 Adam and Eve listened to the lie that they could be like God because they craved what belongs to God alone. In Genesis 11 man again set out on a foolish plan to make a name for himself by building a tower with its top in the heavens. In Romans 1 we learn of the propensity of every human heart to exchange God's truth for a lie and to worship the creature rather than the Creator. Yes, in all of us is a self-centered bent to get me up and to bring God down. There will be no downpour until that sinful inclination is reversed.

At the core of our being is the desire to reduce this thing called holiness so that there's seemingly no separation between us and God. When God is humanized and man is deified, holiness is lost. Everything gets out of perspective. The first step in personal revival is to get God in His rightful place.

When God is recognized as being above me, beyond me, highly exalted, over me, and totally separate from me, I am getting in position for a downpour. When I embrace God for who He is and I understand who I am, and when I know God's place, I can know my place. Then things start to fall into place. That's what God's holiness does for us—it puts everything and everyone in their rightful places.

❸ Which of the following statements describes the view of God needed to prepare us for a downpour? Check one.
- ❏ a. I need to bring God down to my level and see Him as a common, ordinary friend just like me.
- ☑ b. I need to see God in His exalted greatness, holiness, and sovereignty.

Isaiah 6 is the hub for our study on holiness. There Isaiah describes seeing God in His exalted holiness, and his life was forever changed. Isaiah saw the throne room of heaven and was captured by four insights into God's holiness. See for yourself what Isaiah saw and, under the direction of God's Spirit, what he wrote for us in God's Word.

Holiness Describes Separation

Isaiah had a vision of the Lord "in the year that King Uzziah died" (Isa. 6:1). King Uzziah reigned 52 years in the nation of Israel. Imagine the shock waves that would course through our nation if we lost a ruler who had led us for 52 years. Uzziah was the only king most of the people had ever known. When he died, people were wondering who would rule next and what would become of the nation as they had known it. The people were filled with perplexity, fear, and uncertainty.

Heavenly Throne-Room Scene 1: Isaiah 6

It was that year, 740 B.C., when Isaiah saw the Lord. We're not told whether Isaiah was waking or sleeping, in a vision or in a dream, only that he was supernaturally transported to the throne room of the God of the universe. The first words from his mouth in this report of his heavenly visit were "I saw the Lord." John 12:41 tells us that it was actually the preincarnate Christ that Isaiah gazed on in Isaiah 6. No one has seen God, John 1:18 says and continues with, "The only begotten Son, who is in the bosom of the Father, He has declared Him" (NKJV). And so this is Jesus—before Jerusalem, before Nazareth, before Bethlehem. Before He lived in all those places, He was the sovereign Ruler of the universe.

The word translated *Lord* in our English Bibles is lowercase "ord." From the Hebrew language we understand that Isaiah is not using God's personal name, YHWH. Isaiah referred to Him as Lord, meaning, "I saw the One in charge," "I saw the Ruler."

4 **As you read the following description of God on His throne, underline the key truths you learn about God.**

"I saw the Lord *sitting* upon a throne" (emphasis added). Isaiah noted that the Lord was not pacing back and forth. He was not wringing His hands. Remember, God is not like us at all. He was sitting on the throne with no fear, no uncertainty, no anxiety of any kind. In the truest sense God doesn't have a care in the world. God rules the universe with His feet up! You ask, Why does He do that? Because He can; that's why! We're not taxing Him or stretching Him in any way. He's God. He's in charge. He's holy.

"I saw the Lord sitting upon a throne." In a region unknown, in a realm beyond space and time where God is seen and constantly worshiped, in a place we can't go to now but will someday very soon, God's throne is "high and lifted up." This isn't a description of the throne's physical properties. He's not telling us how big the throne is but where it's located in heaven. Why? So even the sinless angels in heaven will understand that God is distinct and uncommon, separate, and holy. Revelation 5:11 tells us that the angels in God's throne room number 10,000 times 10,000, and every one of them is constantly reminded of how completely separate God is because His throne is not on their level; it is "high and lifted up."

Next Isaiah observed that the "train of his robe filled the temple." Married women reading this will have their own stories of wedding dresses that reached to the floor and beyond. Maybe your gown went so far behind that your bridesmaids had to help you move around. Why? Because it was a day to be honored, and the length of the dress was a symbol of splendor.

What does Scripture say about the symbol of God's splendor? The train of His robe didn't just go down the aisle; it "filled the temple"—back and forth, back and forth, doubling and redoubling until the symbol of God's holy splendor packed the house. Over and over the writers of Scripture ask, "Who is like you, O LORD?" (Ex. 15:11; Deut. 33:29; Pss. 35:10; 89:8). The question is rhetorical because the answer is obvious. Who is like God? No one. That's because He is holy. He is separate. He is completely unlike us.

Heavenly Throne-Room Scene 2: Ezekiel 1

Let's go to another throne room in Ezekiel 1 where Ezekiel had a similar revelation of God on the throne. "In the thirtieth year, in the fourth month, on the fifth day of the month ... the heavens were opened, and I saw visions of God ... the word of the LORD came to Ezekiel ... and the hand of the Lord was upon him there" (vv. 1-4). Ezekiel went on for 21 verses to describe everything he saw in heaven except God Himself. He saved the best for last.

⑤ Now read about Ezekiel's description of God on His throne. Underline the key truths you learn about God.

Ezekiel 1:26 says, "Above the expanse over their heads there was the likeness of a throne." Anyone who's ever been to heaven talks about the throne, as we will see. "There was the likeness of a throne, in appearance like sapphire; and seated above the likeness of a throne was a likeness with a human appearance." It's interesting that in this section of Scripture, Ezekiel uses the word *likeness* 10 times and the word *appearance* 16 times. He describes what he sees as, sort of like ... a bit of ... kind of like. He does his best, but cannot find the words for what he sees, and neither would we.

Isaiah 40:25 says, "To whom then will you compare me, that I should be like him?" There is nothing to compare to the Lord. He's holy. Our words amount to a heap of inadequate comparisons ... and I'm trying to ... but I can't come close ... to describing ... God. Ezekiel continues:

> *Upward from what had the appearance of his waist I saw as it were gleaming metal, like the appearance of fire enclosed all around. And downward from what had the appearance of his waist I saw as it were the appearance of fire, and there was brightness around him. Like the appearance of the bow that is in the cloud on the day of rain, so was the appearance of the brightness all around. Such was the appearance of the likeness of the glory of the LORD. And when I saw it, I fell on my face*
> **Ezekiel 1:27-28**

Ezekiel was saying, "When I saw it, I had to get down low. God is high, and when I saw how exalted He is, I had to get as far from Him as possible." Why? Holiness. Holiness shouts separation. He's lofty and exalted, and we're not. You are at all like God. Get as low as you can, as soon as possible. He is holy!

Take a moment before you continue and get low before the Lord. Envision Him in His awesome holiness and worship before Him.

Now that is a view of God that we have lost in the church in our generation: the high, exalted, lofty, exclusive, unparalleled, unprecedented character of God. Preferring the comfort of His nearness, we have lost the reality of God's transcendent holiness. Our generation struggles and wallows in cheap grace and shallow sanctification because we have departed from the biblical picture of God's holy and exalted nature. God is not the "Man upstairs" or "Big Daddy" or some old codger with a long, white beard. God is not whatever my conscience or imagination would like Him to be. God is indescribable glory, and He dwells in unapproachable light. "God is a consuming fire" (Heb. 12:29). In a single word: holy! God is infinite holiness.

Pray that God will continue to reveal His holiness to the church and the world in our generation. Pray that God's people will get a correct view of Him that will help us see ourselves as He sees us.

day 2 | Holiness Demands Caution

Holiness rightly understood demands caution. Do you get it? *Be careful.* Be very careful. Isaiah has briefly described the position of the throne and the clothing of deity, but he really doesn't say anything about God Himself. Not really. He tells you about where the throne is and the train of His robe; and then he's, like, speechless, out of breath, afraid to say more. As a result, Isaiah's description moves abruptly to "Let me tell you about the angels."

Isaiah 6:2 says, "Above him stood the seraphim." Seraphim are angels, literally the burning ones. Apparently, they appear next to God as fire. What are they doing? They're standing, ever standing to serve the seated Sovereign.

Next Isaiah tells us "each had six wings." He focuses now on a specific seraphim. "With two [wings] he covered his face," lest they gaze on infinite holiness and be consumed in a moment. "And with two he covered his feet." Why? So that God would not see them.

Revelation 19:12 tells us that the Lord's eyes are "like a flame of fire." No wonder the seraphim cover themselves. They don't want to look at God, and they don't want God to look at them. *Holiness, gazing at me? Not if I can help it.* But I can't. Even though the seraphim are sinless, they don't want heaven's holiest eyes falling on their forms. "With two he covered his face, and with two he covered his feet, and with two he flew." Ever serving, never seeing this sovereign God. Their motion is ceaseless as they do the bidding of Almighty God.

You can't read verse 2 without sensing in the seraphim a consuming carefulness around God. "Caution! Caution! Do what He says, exactly, immediately, totally, every time. He's God; we're not. He's holy; fly right. Don't look at Him. Cover yourself. Holiness! Caution! Holiness demands caution."

1 Suppose you were given the assignment to write the text for a caution sign just outside the door to God's throne room. What would you say to people who were about to enter?

CAUTION: ______________________________

____

Heavenly Throne-Room Scene 3

Let's go to another throne-room scene and see the same thing. At the absolute end of human history, we are not surprised to find God's throne unaffected, unaltered. We enter John's vision in Revelation near the end of history. Now he refers to God's throne room again but in a scene I hope you never witness. John describes the dead, both small and great, who are outside Christ, standing before God at the final judgment.

Revelation 20:11 says, "I saw a great white throne and him who was seated on it. From his presence earth and sky fled away, and no place was found for them." It's still there, eternal and immovable—God's throne. The whiteness is a picture of purity. It's the same term Mark used in chapter 9 to describe Jesus at the transfiguration: "Exceedingly white, as no launderer on earth can whiten" (Mark 9:3, NASB). The earth sees holiness and retreats. The sky sees holiness and pulls back.

What happens when holiness really hits home in the human heart? Second Peter 3:10 describes this time: "The day of the Lord will come like a thief, and then the heavens will pass away with a roar, and the heavenly bodies will be burned up and dissolved, and the earth and the works that are done on it will be exposed." The point clearly is, Caution. When God is recognized for the infinitely holy Being that He is, you don't stand around questioning His decisions. You run and hide. You get as far away and as low as you can, as fast as you can. That's God.

It always grieves me when I hear people say, "Well, if I ever meet God, I'm going to tell Him a thing or two." What are you talking about? Step away from me when you say stuff like that. Do we have any idea what we're talking about? Not if we aren't filled with fear and awful dread when we think about a genuine encounter with the God who made us all and spoke the very universe into existence.

No one questions God. Does God do some things we don't understand? Yes. Does God do some things we wish were different? Yes. But isn't there something inside us that says, "I'm human, I'm fallible, I'm sinful. I don't know what's ultimately best. I don't understand how it all fits together or even what God is trying to do in a given situation." Instead, I must choose to trust God. Often I say to myself, *I trust the Lord. He's awesome, He's holy. He knows what He's doing, and He's doing it perfectly, on time, every time.* Eternity will show the infinite, unfathomable wisdom of our almighty, holy God. You may be tempted to think, *Well, He's sure doing things differently than I would do them.* Right. Remember our definition? *Holy* means not like us.

Speaking of the day when humanity meets holiness, Luke 23:30 says, "Then they will begin to say to the mountains, 'Fall on us,' and to the hills, 'Cover us.'" Hiding—or trying to hide—is, of course, complete futility. Rightly seen, holiness makes you want to cover yourself. Holiness rightly understood says, "Caution, extreme caution" when talking about, thinking about, and living before a God like that.

Conclude today's lesson in prayer. Imagine your life standing side by side with God's purity and whiteness. Confess to Him anything you see that discolors your life and hides His glory. ↑

Activate

The content for today's lesson is short. I want you to get alone with God and acknowledge His holiness.

1 Prepare yourself by reviewing one or more of the throne-room scenes we've already studied. Begin by readying Isaiah 6:1-10. Pay attention to Isaiah's response to God's holiness. If you want to review the others, read Ezekiel 1 and Revelation 20:11-15.

2 Get completely alone with God. Shut off anything that could distract you. Close all doors. If you are physically able, get on your face before God—lie flat on the floor. This isn't the time to make any requests of God. Now is the time to humble yourself before Him, acknowledging His holiness. Think about His purity, righteousness, and holiness.

Tell Him in your own words, "I now see You, Lord, high and lifted up, beyond any previous image I had of You. I worship You in the beauty of Your holiness. How great You are—how completely beyond anything of this world. Why do You even think of me? Help me grasp what it's like to come into the presence of Your holiness."

3 Stay in this prayer position longer than is comfortable. Ask God to help you keep your focus on Him. When you face up to God's holiness, you find yourself facedown in worship.

4 After your time before the Lord, write a prayer to Him or a poem about His holiness:

Holy, holy, holy is the Lord God Almighty ...

_____

_____

_____

_____

_____

_____

_____

downpour

day 4 | Break Up Your Fallow Ground

Hosea 10:12 explains that in part, pressing on to know the Lord means we examine our hearts for places God needs to revive: "Sow for yourselves righteousness; reap steadfast love; *break up your fallow ground*, for it is the time to seek the Lord, that he may come and rain righteousness upon you" (emphasis added).

❶ Why would it be important to sow righteousness, reap love, and break up ground in order to be ready to seek the Lord?

---

❷ What do you think it means for God to "rain righteousness upon you"?

Its a pouring out of His love + grace

Fallow ground is land that has not been seeded for one or more growing seasons. It is hard and may be filled with weeds. It is undeveloped but potentially useful. In order to plant seed and reap a bountiful harvest, you must break it up, plow it, and prepare it to receive the seed. Hosea is not talking about land; he's talking about your life. Today I want you to focus on your potentially fallow ground.

❸ Consider the areas of your life that are fallow—areas that have become dry and dead. As you prepare for personal revival, ask yourself these questions. If the question prompts you to identify "fallow ground" in your life, write below it something you can begin doing to plow it up and make it more receptive and responsive to God's work in your life.

1. Is prayer a vital part of my life?
   ☑ Yes   ❏ Not really   ❏ Not as much as it needs to be or used to be

---

2. Am I hungry for God's Word? Do I want to go deeper in my heart-understanding of what God has for me in His Word?
   ☑ Yes   ❏ Not really   ❏ Not as much as I need to

---

3. Does the reality of heaven and hell move me to action in sharing Christ with family, friends, and coworkers who are headed to a Christless eternity and eternal separation from God?
   ❏ Yes   ❏ Not really   ☑ Not as much as it needs to

Week 2: God on the Throne, Part 1

4. Am I ever concerned that I'm missing out on some things God would like to do in my life?
❑ Yes ☑ Sometimes ❑ No

---

5. Is my thinking dominated by my desire to be more like Christ, or am I mostly preoccupied with acquiring money/goods?
❑ More like Christ ❑ ~~More money/goods~~ *healthcare need.*

Both

---

6. Can I watch degrading movies and television and read morally inappropriate literature and not be deeply grieved in my heart and shut it off or walk away?
☑ Yes, sometimes ❑ No

---

7. Do I have a pet sin, in thought or behavior, that I refuse to confront and surrender in obedience to the Lord? Do I let myself off the hook for my sin and laziness by saying that the Lord understands? Did I used to feel more convicted about it than I do now?
❑ Yes ❑ Not that I know of

---

8. Do pointed spiritual discussions make me feel embarrassed or cynical?
❑ Sometimes ☑ No

---

9. How long has it been since I felt true joy?
❑ Can't remember when ❑ A long time ☑ Recently, but I want more!

---

10. Am I dissatisfied with the level of my intimacy with God?
❑ Yes ❑ No, not really
I want more

---

11. Am I willing to do what it takes to break up fallow ground in my life and aggressively deal with sin that I know about in order to experience afresh the Lord's power and presence?
☑ Yes, I want this with all my heart, more than anything else.
❏ Yes, but I'm a bit scared of what this will mean.
❏ Uncertain, depends on what it will cost me.
❏ Uncertain, not sure if/how it will work.

Pray and ask the Lord to develop in your life a willingness to do everything necessary to be ready to receive everything He wants to sow and rain down on your life. Review the previous questions and express to the Lord your desire for change in these areas. ⊤

day 5 | Hezekiah's Personal Revival

❶ Read about the picture of personal revival from the life of Hezekiah on page 34. As time permits, read one or more of the biblical accounts in 2 Kings 18–20; 2 Chronicles 29–32; and Isaiah 36–39. If you read only one, choose 2 Chronicles 29–32.

❷ Review the pattern of Hezekiah's leadership of the people in returning to the Lord.
1. Hezekiah and the Levites purified themselves and the temple. Then they restored proper worship (see 2 Chron. 29).
2. Hezekiah issued a call to gather in Jerusalem and celebrate the Passover, and "the hand of God was also on Judah to give them one heart to do what the king and the princes commanded by the word of the Lord" (2 Chron. 30:12).
3. The revived worshipers "went out to the cities of Judah and broke in pieces the pillars and cut down the Asherim and broke down the high places and the altars" (2 Chron. 31:1).

Pray and ask the Lord to stir your heart and the hearts of your fellow church members to—
• come clean before the Lord and fix your eyes on Him in genuine worship;
• return to obedience in the things clearly commanded by the Lord;
• remove all impurities around you that do not reflect the holiness of the God you love and serve.

From the Life of Hezekiah: A Picture of God's Holiness

2 KINGS 18–20; 2 CHRONICLES 29–32; ISAIAH 36–39

The multiple chapters of the Bible dedicated to the life and times of Hezekiah move like the plot line of a great war movie. There's the humble hero facing insurmountable odds against enemy armies. Just when you think there's no way out, the plot twists, and good triumphs over evil. When the credits roll, you shake your head, amazed that the real hero of the story is "Almighty God—the Holy One of Israel," once again rescuing and blessing the people who are called by His name. None of the earthly empires who came up against God's people could stand against the One who sits on the throne of the universe.

Hezekiah, Israel's king who did what was right in the eyes of the Lord (see 2 Chron. 29:2), was one of the first kings in many decades to have a proper understanding of a holy God on the throne of heaven. The bumper sticker on his royal limo could have read, "Fear nothing but God and sin," and he lived by that rule.

Hezekiah's heavenly perspective made him quick to bow to God's authority on earth. He dedicated his life to cleaning up God's house and leading God's people back to the priority of worship and holiness. Without personal holiness, true worship is impossible. The priests in the temple repented in shame when they realized how their behavior had dishonored a holy God. This deep work of confession and repentance led to great joy in the people's newfound forgiveness. God's highway of holiness is the only road by which the downpour of God's blessing can reach us.

Hezekiah saw people who had previously not had the time or inclination to celebrate the Passover and regular times in the temple now rush to God's house. They couldn't stay away. Revival had breathed new life into what had become mechanical. Because they were convinced that the holy God of Israel was present in their midst, their worship overflowed with a reverent awe of their Creator God.

"God is for us!" Hezekiah's confidence never shook despite the threatening, turbulent times. And the people could not hold back their worship when they traced their victory in battle back to God's promise to reward their personal persistence in fighting sin in their lives. Hezekiah's desire was to do all things for the praise of God's glory. That commitment not only protected them against their enemies but also brought revival to their souls. ↑

downpour

God on the throne: a picture of holiness

PART 2

God on the throne: a picture of holiness

PART 2

key verse to memorize

*"As he who called you is holy, you also be holy
in all your conduct."*

1 Peter 1:15

For session 3 plans, turn to page 170 in the leader guide.

discussion guide on week 2: God on the throne, part 1

1. What first comes to your mind when you think about God? (activity 1, p. 24)
2. What are the key truths you've learned about God from the throne-room scenes in Isaiah 6 and Ezekiel 1 (pp. 26–27)?
3. What words of caution would you give someone who was about to enter the throne room of heaven (activity 1, p. 28)?
4. How do the earth and sky react to God's holiness in Revelation 20:11? How should humans react in the presence of God's holiness?
5. Suppose someone said in your presence, "If I ever meet God, I'm going to tell Him a thing or two." What caution would you offer him or her?
6. Volunteers, share your poem from page 30.

dvd session 3 message notes (38 minutes)

Scripture focus: Isaiah 6:1-4

3. Holiness declares ___glory___ (Isa. 6:3).
    • The whole earth is full of His glory.
    • The weather systems are full of His glory.
    • The solar system and the universe are full of His glory.
    • The human body is full of His glory.
    Throne room 4—John's heavenly vision (Rev. 4:1-11)
4. Holiness determines ___MYSTERY___ (Isa. 6:4).
    • Holiness says this far and no farther.
    • Mystery continues until the trumpet sounds (Rev. 10:4-7).
    • In eternity we will see Him as He is (1 John 3:2).
    Throne room 5—Daniel 7:9-10
    • The book of life was opened (Rev. 20:11-15).
    • Some need a true conversion. Some need to turn. Others need to return.

downpour

snapshot summary

God is holy, and the whole universe reveals His glory. Yet our knowledge of Him is still limited by mystery. But revival starts here.

my goals for you

I want you to understand the glory and mystery surrounding God's holiness and to show your reverent fear of Him in your prayers and in your lifestyle.

Message music: see the "The Glory of God" lyrics on page 38.

responding to the message

1. Review by answering the following questions:
   a. What evidence of God's glory causes the greatest awe in your thinking and why?
   b. What have you learned about God and His throne room from John's vision and Daniel's vision?
   c. What is the purpose of the books that will be opened in heaven?
2. Confess to the Lord in prayer the truths you've learned about His holiness and His glory. Express your awe, reverence, and adoration to Him.
3. Close with a prayer that every individual will come to an assurance about his or her name being found in the book of life.

preview statements for this week's study

- God stood in eternity past and spoke, and the worlds were formed (see Heb. 11:3). Who is like You, O Lord?
- Our intricately designed bodies are shouting the workmanship of a Master Designer.
- God doesn't share His glory. "Not to us, O LORD ... but to your name give glory" (Ps. 115:1).
- Sincere worship, given from the heart, is never over the top, or too much, because He is worthy.
- In our humanness we can't handle all His holiness; so God, in mercy, raises the veil and dwells in mystery.
- Ask yourself the questions, *Are my hands clean? Is my heart pure?*

Message-notes blanks: glory, mystery

The Glory of God

Creator God from ages past / the living One, the first and last
You are the Lord of all eternity / the God who is and always was
the world is only here because
the word You spoke brought everything to be
and when You speak again that day / the earth and sky will melt away
and we'll see you in Your glory

the glory of God, the glory of God
Your people bow down;
we're casting our crowns / before Your throne
the glory of God, the glory of God
our voices proclaim praise to the name
of God alone, the glory of God

and when You come upon the clouds
and all the creatures cry out loud / Hallelujah to our Lord and King!
then You will gather all your own / away to our eternal home
where songs of everlasting joy we'll sing / and there our tears will all be gone
in heaven's bright majestic dawn / where Your glory shines forever

so every moment, every day / everything I do and say
i'm living only to display Your glory

*"Whether you eat or drink, or whatever you do,
do all to the glory of God."*
1 Corinthians 10:31

"The twenty-four elders fall down before him who is seated on the throne and worship him who lives forever and ever. They cast their crowns before the throne, saying, Worthy are you, our Lord and God, to receive glory and honor and power, for you created all things, and by your will they existed and were created."
Revelation 4:10-11

Read the lyrics above and meditate on the meaning of this song. This week listen to the song on your Message-Music CD (track 2) and meditate on the glory of God as He sits on His throne.

Tell God all the things you see and know about Him that reveal His glory.

Holiness Declares God's Glory

Isaiah 6:3 describes the activity of the seraphim: "One called to another and said: 'Holy, holy, holy is the LORD of hosts; the whole earth is full of his glory!'" This is the chorus that has been going on through eons of time. It's happening in heaven right now and will never cease.

Think of all the things God could have chosen to say about Himself in His presence. God could have called on the seraphim to sing, "Loving, loving, loving God," and it would have been true. They could chorus, "Merciful, merciful, merciful," and we would say, "Amen." I'm guessing, though, that the seraphim probably don't have a ton of autonomy around God's throne. I'm pretty sure they do exactly what God commands them to do. Do you agree? What is spoken in God's presence is what God most wants said and seen and understood about Himself. Those words and nothing else, ever!

God has deemed that the central, defining characteristic of His being—the word that is to be spoken in heaven eternally and continuously, the characteristic around which all other aspects of God's nature revolve—is this: holiness. Isaiah describes two angelic lines coming out from the throne, and one called to another. Two lines calling out back and forth, back and forth, back and forth—an antiphonal chorus that never ceases.

In the Hebrew language repetition shows force. In Scripture several of God's attributes are used twice. But only regarding this attribute and only here and in Revelation 4:8 do we see this three-peat. It's saying that God is not just holy. God is not just holy-holy. God is holy-holy-holy!

1 **Fill in the blanks from last week's memory verse, Isaiah 6:3.**

"Holy, _____, holy is the _____ of hosts;

the whole _____ is full of his _____!"

The Universe Declares God's Glory

There is no place you can go and nothing your eyes can gaze on that isn't this moment declaring the fact of God's existence and His exaltation over what He has made. All created things shout the Creator's existence. God's glory is revealed because He made it. Let's think about that for a moment.

The weather system is full of His glory. Think of the awesome energy of Hurricane Katrina. Scientists tell us that Katrina's energy was comparable to 20 times the energy of the bomb that was dropped on Hiroshima. Extreme weather is measured in the thousands of people it kills, the millions who go without power, and the hundreds of billions of dollars it will take to repair the ravaged area of our country. No wonder they're called acts of God. Storms are, of course, a muted display of God's glory. The engine that drives those kinds of storms is only a fractional representation of God's reality. It's a manifestation of holy power that performs these things on this tiny sphere we call earth.

The earth is full of His glory. Some would think that God isn't taking care of the world, but how wrong it is to think that. Did you know that the earth's axis is perfectly situated for life on this earth? Our planet sits at an angle of 23 degrees in relation to the sun. If that were adjusted just slightly, the climate on the earth would be drastically different. Life as we know it would be difficult or nonexistent without God to maintain this angle.

Our solar system is full of His glory. Our sun is so massive that it could fit 1.3 million of our earths inside it. It may not look that big, but it is. It hangs in space 93 million miles away from us—and that's just in our solar system. The Bible says that God sustains the universe. By His power all things are created and sustained. Colossians 1:17 says, "In him all things hold together." The earth and our solar system are full of His glory.

The universe is full of His glory. Our galaxy, the Milky Way, is so expansive that it would take one thousand lifetimes traveling at the speed of light just to cross it. And relatively speaking, all of this stuff is in our backyard. Astronomers number galaxies at 140 billion in the universe. (Yeah, as if they counted them.) Can we imagine how many a billion is? No, it's really beyond our comprehension. It would take 140 billion peas to fill Chicago's Soldier Field Stadium, with every single pea representing a galaxy. Our solar system is only a tiny part of just one galaxy. God stood in eternity past and spoke, and the worlds were formed (see Heb. 11:3). Who is like you, O Lord?

Forget the Telescope; Look in the Mirror

Augustine, one of the church fathers, rightly observed that "men go abroad to wonder at the height of mountains, at the huge waves of the sea, at the long courses of the river, at the vast compass of the ocean, at the circle motion of the stars; and they pass by themselves without wondering at all." The human body declares the glory of God with greater volume than a galaxy ever could.

What God has created in the human body staggers the mind. Each of us has one hundred thousand miles of blood vessels—enough to reach around the earth three times. Our hearts beat one hundred thousand times every day. (You probably aren't even working on that; yet it is still happening right now, thank God.) A three-month-old unborn baby already has detailed fingerprints. It's true what Psalm 139:14 says: We are "fearfully and wonderfully made." Our intricately designed bodies are shouting the workmanship of a Master Designer.

❷ What aspect of God's glory wows you the most? Check one.
  ❏ a. Weather systems and the earth
  ❏ b. The solar system and the universe
  ❏ c. The human body

Why? _____

_____

Can you keep the earth perfectly tilted? Can you keep the planets and the stars moving in a galactic choreography? Can you do that? If God said, "I'm not doing it anymore," could you suggest someone who might take over for Him? There is no one like Him. He is holy. He is unparalleled. He is unprecedented.

He is first, and no one else even rates a distant second. Words fail in helping us comprehend the unalterable, incomprehensible holiness of God. How right the seraphim are to be singing this moment, "Holy, holy, holy is the LORD of hosts; the whole earth is full of his glory." Everywhere we turn, we see the fingerprints of God.

> **Describe to God the things that most reveal His glory to you. Be specific from the microscopic to the galactic. List things in the margin that cause you to stand in awe of His greatness.** ✝

day 2 | Heavenly Throne-Room Scene 4

Today let me take you to another throne-room scene. In Revelation John describes a heavenly vision that includes a view into God's throne room.

❶ Turn to Revelation 4:1-5 in your Bible. As you read, look for the things John describes in this throne room that are similar to the other scenes we've studied. Write the similarities below.

_____

Notice the similarities of this description to the other scenes: the throne, God seated, the rainbow, heavenly creatures, fire, and flashing light. John too is having difficulty with words that are adequate to describe what he sees. Jasper and carnelian were the most precious jewels of John's day. He's comparing the Lord to these. Then *seven spirits of God?* Who is that?

Some suggest that the number seven in Scripture is a picture of fullness or completeness, as in Daniel's reference to 70 days in Daniel 9:24. Others believe the seven spirits refer to Isaiah 11:2: "The Spirit of the LORD shall rest upon him, the Spirit of wisdom and understanding, the Spirit of counsel and might, the Spirit of knowledge and the fear of the LORD."

❷ Now read Revelation 4:6-11. What characteristic of God do you read that is repeated three times to indicate force?

_____

Does this remind you of Isaiah 6? It should. This is the same throne room! Why off with the crowns? Because no one, rightly viewing God's holy throne room, wants to be associated with personal honor. God doesn't share His glory. "Not to us, O LORD ... but to your name give glory" (Ps. 115:1).

John also adds to our understanding of the angelic chorus: "Worthy are you, our Lord and God" (Rev. 4:11). The word translated *worthy* was used of properly balanced scales. If the weight of the precious metal was equivalent to the standard weight, it was considered worthy—it balanced out. When

Scripture says God is worthy, it means there is no amount of praise that we can place on Him that somehow tips the scales. We can't come close to overdoing our expression of praise and worship.

Sincere worship, given from the heart, is never over the top, or too much, because He is worthy. *"Worthy* are you, our Lord and God, to receive glory and honor and power, for you created all things, and by your will they existed and were created" (Rev. 4:11, emphasis added).

Listen again to "The Glory of God" and sing along if you like. Focus your attention on bowing and casting a crown before the Lord in worship.

Name to God things of great value and declare that He is more worthy than every thing of value you can imagine. Make a list in the margin. ↑

day 3 | Holiness Determines Mystery

Holiness describes separation. It demands caution. It declares glory. And finally, holiness determines mystery.

Let's return to Isaiah 6: "The foundations of the thresholds shook at the voice of him who called, and the house was filled with smoke" (v. 4). Isaiah, at the door to the throne room, no doubt prostrate by now, feels the entire room begin to shake as the Lord speaks. What the Lord said we do not know, but it must have been a call for the vision to end, because Isaiah's vision is immediately shrouded by smoke.

If you're like me, you have to wonder why all the shaking? Why the smoke? Why the audible call that the audience must end? Here's why: holiness always says, "This far; no farther. This close; no closer. This part you get to know; this part though you can't even comprehend." There's always a mystery at the center of holiness. Inevitably, God sets up a perimeter and halts our progress on the outskirts of holiness.

In Revelation 10:4-7 John was writing like mad everything the Spirit showed him. Suddenly the Lord gave the command "Do not write it down." John may have thought, *Well, I just saw it, and I want to write it down.* "No, don't!" God has placed limits on what He wants us to know about Him. Revelation 10 goes on to describe the day when the trumpet will sound and all mystery will be revealed. Someday Christ will return, and those who love the Lord will go to be with Him. Only then will the mystery be removed. "Then [we] shall know fully, even as [we] have been fully known," says 1 Corinthians 13:12. It will be a time promised in 1 John 3:2: "We shall be like him, because we shall see him as he is."

For now, however, as long as we're living on earth, as long as we're in these imperfect bodies, there will be a certain amount of mystery. This far and no farther—that's why Isaiah saw the foundations shaking, heard the voice calling out, and saw the house filling with smoke. That's it—no more.

Mystery. In our humanness we can't handle all His holiness; so God, in mercy, raises the veil and dwells in mystery.

> Pause and thank God for all He reveals about Himself and tell Him of your willingness to accept the mystery about the things you can't know or understand.

Heavenly Throne-Room Scene 5

Now we'll visit that final throne room that confirms the reality—no, the necessity—of mystery. Daniel is the other human messenger who was given a view of this holy throne room. Daniel 7:9 begins, "As I looked, thrones were placed, and the Ancient of days took his seat; his clothing was white as snow." Have you noticed how these scenes of the throne room are somewhat similar? Isn't it interesting that the writers of Scripture, living hundreds of years apart—men who never knew one another and most of whom didn't even read one another's writings—all report the very same things? Why is that? Because what they were seeing is real, and they were really seeing it.

> *"The hair of his head like pure wool; his throne was fiery flames; its wheels were burning fire. [Mystery!] A stream of fire issued and came out from before him, [Mystery!] a thousand thousands served him, and ten thousand times ten thousand stood before him; [Mystery!] the court sat in judgment, and the books were opened."*
> **Daniel 7:9-10**

The Book of Life

You may wonder, *What books?* You definitely need to know about the books. Revelation 20 explains: "I saw a great white throne and him who was seated on it. From his presence earth and sky fled away, and no place was found for them. And I saw the dead, great and small, standing before the throne, and books were opened. Then another book was opened, which is the book of life. ... And if anyone's name was not found written in the book of life, he was thrown into the lake of fire" (vv. 11-12,15).

1 Answer the following questions about this throne-room scene.

1. Who was standing before the throne? _____

2. What was the name of this final book? The book of _____

3. What will happen to those whose names are not written in the book of life?

_____

4. Has your name already been written in that book?   ❏ Yes   ❏ No

Careful! Keep in mind that your name is not in the book of life just because you say it's there. Your name is in the book of life because you meet the soul conditions for the new birth. Have you recognized your sinful, fallen condition before a holy God? Have you turned from your sin, rejecting that old lifestyle, and given your life to Jesus Christ and to Him alone? Can you say from your heart that He is your reason for living now? Has He become to you everything you love and long for, your very reason for life itself? That's what it means to be transformed by the power of the gospel. Now allow me to ask again:

② Is your name in the book of life? Check one.
   ❏ a. Yes, I've turned from sin, I've trusted Christ, and He has changed me!
   ❏ b. No, I'm afraid I'm still in that fallen and sinful condition without Christ.
   ❏ c. I'm still not sure. Can you help me?

You can't fool God. If He's not the "pearl of great value" to you (Matt. 13:46), if He's not the treasure of your affection in increasing measure, then your name is not in the book. Matthew 7:22-23 says that many people will say on that day, "Lord, Lord, did we not prophesy in your name, and cast out demons in your name, and do many mighty works in your name?" And Jesus will say, "I never knew you; depart from me."

You don't know the Lord because you say you do or because your mom says you do or because your pastor says you do. You can be sure you know the Lord when your life, your behavior, your actions, and your attitudes confirm that you do. "If anyone is in Christ, he is a new creation. The old has passed away; behold, the new has come" (2 Cor. 5:17).

There are no perfect people reading or writing this, but we must be people who are changing day by day. Our testimonies should be "I don't talk to my wife the way I used to. I don't go where I used to go. I stopped looking at things that made me feel guilty and ashamed. I used to be addicted to a certain substance that calmed my nerves and took the edge off; now I'm in Christ, and there is no edge. I am free from what used to enslave me. I'm free in Christ. The power of sin is broken in me, and I'm changing day by day by day. My language is different, my thoughts are higher, my priorities are better, my purpose is beyond myself. I've been born again."

That's the story of a person whose name is in the book of life. Is that your story? Is your name in that book? If not, you're not ready to stand before a holy God. You must turn. By faith turn from sin and to God.

③ If you know your present destiny is that lake of fire described in Revelation 20, you can turn around right now. Turn back to page 18 and choose this new relationship with Jesus Christ right now.

If you know and love the Lord, never let God's holiness get far from your focus. Remember who He really is and what it means to account to this God of infinite, indescribable holiness.

  Pray that God will draw many to faith in His Son Jesus so that their names will be recorded in the book of life. ⭡

| # The First Great Awakening

The Great Awakening in America happened during the 1730s and 1740s. Conversions in the colonies increased more than fourfold. You've already read about one of the key men whom God used during the Great Awakening —Jonathan Edwards. He was tall and thin and unimpressive in his oratory skills, reading his hour-long sermons to his congregation from his notes. Yet he possessed a deep, profound belief in the holiness of God and the reality of hell for any person who would pass into eternity without Jesus Christ.

His most famous sermon was "Sinners in the Hands of an Angry God." The point of his message was to awaken people to the utmost holiness of God and the need to be reconciled with Him. During the sermon sinners in the audience groaned, pleaded for him to stop preaching, and even fainted among them as they listened. An eyewitness reported, "Before the sermon was done there was a great moaning and crying throughout the whole house. 'What shall I do to be saved? Oh, I'm going to hell! What shall I do for Christ?' The minister was obliged to desist, the shrieks and the cries were so piercing."

Here is a brief quotation from that sermon. Be patient with the old style of writing and read it for its message:

① As you read, circle or underline statements that are particularly striking.

The wrath of God is like great waters that are dammed for the present; they increase more and more, and rise higher and higher, till an outlet is given; and the longer the stream is stopped, the more rapid and mighty is its course, when once it is let loose. It is true, that judgment against your evil works has not been executed hitherto; the floods of God's vengeance have been withheld; but your guilt in the mean time is constantly increasing, and you are every day treasuring up more wrath; the waters are constantly rising, and waxing more and more mighty; and there is nothing but the mere pleasure of God, that holds the waters back, that are unwilling to be stopped, and press hard to go forward. If God should only withdraw his hand from the flood-gate, it would immediately fly open, and the fiery floods of the fierceness and wrath of God would rush forth with inconceivable fury, and would come upon you with omnipotent power; and if your strength were ten thousand times greater than it is, yea, ten thousand times greater than the strength of the stoutest, sturdiest devil in hell, it would be nothing to withstand or endure it.

The bow of God's wrath is bent, and the arrow made ready on the string, and justice bends the arrow at your heart, and strains the bow, and it is nothing but the mere pleasure of God, and that of an angry God, without any promise or obligation at all, that keeps the arrow one moment from being made drunk with your blood. Thus all you that never passed under a great change of heart, by the mighty power of the Spirit of God upon your souls; all you that were never born again, and made new creatures, and raised from being dead in sin, to a state of new, and before altogether unexperienced light and life, are in the hands of an angry God. However you may have reformed your life in many things, and may have had religious affections, and may keep up a form of religion in your families and closets, and in the house of God, it is nothing but his mere pleasure that keeps you from being this moment swallowed up in everlasting destruction. However unconvinced you may now be of the truth of what you hear, by and by you will be fully convinced of it. Those that are gone from being in the like circumstances with you, see that it was so with them; for destruction came suddenly upon most of them; when they expected nothing of it, and while they were saying, Peace and safety: now they see, that those things on which they depended for peace and safety were nothing but thin air and empty shadows. [For a full text of "Sinners in the Hands of an Angry God" visit the Jonathan Edwards Center at Yale on the Internet at *http://edwards.yale.edu/*.]

This is what God's holiness means to us right now. You cannot fool Him, trick Him, or play games with Him as we are tempted to do at times. God is holy; He is not like us. You may have a way of getting out of jams, using your skill with words or your winsome way. Such approaches are worthless before the holy God who made you. He perfectly knows the true condition of your soul.

Some need to turn from sin, and self, and pleasure-seeking, and "look at me; aren't I a good boy?" and reputation and self-consuming godlessness. Turn from these empty things and embrace Christ by faith as the great treasure of your soul. Turn.

For those who have made that turn and have experienced life in Christ, hear with me the call to *return*. Come, let us return to the Lord as the great object of our life and affections. Let us return to the God of infinite holiness.

Gather up in your mind, in your heart, and in your strength what the Lord has been saying to you as you have read this week. Keep in mind that the Word of God is a seed that has been planted in your spirit today. The Bible says the enemy would come to snatch away the seed that has been sown in your heart. You could have it out of your mind before you close this book. But God's desire is that this seed will be nurtured with further meditation, prayer, reflection, and study so that it might grow up into life and faith and obedience to Him. This is where revival begins. God on the throne: a picture of holiness.

Replicate: Giving Glory to Your Holy God
I want you to talk with someone about what you have learned about God's holiness during the past two weeks.

2 **Choose one of the following to spend time with in person or on the phone. Try to complete this assignment before your small-group session.**
❑ One of your children and/or your spouse
❑ A close friend, neighbor, coworker, or relative

3 **Explain that you have been studying about five visions of God's throne room in heaven and you've been given an assignment to tell someone what you've learned. (This is that assignment!) Include in your sharing some of the following or share other things that have been meaningful.**

1. Describe God's throne room and the parts of the visions that are similar. You can read or tell their stories. Invite children to try and color a picture of one of the throne-room scenes.
2. Describe the difficulties Isaiah, Ezekiel, John, and Daniel had trying to put in human words the glory of what they saw.
3. Explain what *holiness* is. Then describe how heavenly beings and humans respond in the presence of God's holiness.
4. Give some examples of God's glory and/or describe His mystery.
5. Tell them about the book of life, whose names are written in it, and what happens to those whose names are not included.
6. Explain the value and need of turning to Christ or returning to Him.
7. Close your time in prayer.

Elevate

Pray the following prayer or use words of your own to worship the Lord.
Lord, thank You for a fresh view of Your exalted, holy nature. Great God of the universe, holy and high, lifted up, I exalt You, Lord. You are the object of my greatest thoughts, the end of my deepest affections. I give myself wholly to You and to You alone. Revive me according to Your Word even as I bow. I ask in Jesus' strong name. Amen. ✝

day 5 | Personal Revival in Scotland

1 Read about the picture of personal revival in Scotland on page 48. Pay attention to the role prayer and personal preparation had in leading to a significant move of God on the island of Lewis.

2 If you have access to the Internet and time permits, conduct a search for "Duncan Campbell" and find one of his testimonies of this revival in an MP3 format. Download it and listen to this firsthand testimony of revival. This revival is often called the Hebrides Revival or the Lewis Awakening. The testimony may also be found in text form as "When the Mountains Flowed Down" by Duncan Campbell.

Ask yourself the questions, *Are my hands clean? Is my heart pure?* and respond to the Lord in prayer. Then claim the promise: "I will pour water on the thirsty land, and streams on the dry ground" (Isa. 43:3). Pray for a downpour. Better yet, get together with one or more other believers and plead with God for an outpouring of His Spirit.

Clean Hands and Pure Hearts— Revival in Scotland (1949)

In 1949 two elderly women prayed daily for revival in their lives and in the Hebrides Islands of Scotland. Faith had reached a low point in their country. They were so spiritually thirsty that they claimed God's promise

"I will pour water on the thirsty land, and streams on the dry ground."

Isaiah 44:3

They convinced their pastor that people should ask God to quicken their hearts. He and a handful of men gathered in a barn nightly for prayer for months but with no results. Then one day, early in the morning hours, a young man read Psalm 24:3-5:

"Who shall ascend the hill of the LORD?
  And who shall stand in his holy place?
He who has clean hands and a pure heart,
  who does not lift up his soul to what
    is false
  and does not swear deceitfully.
He will receive blessing from the LORD
  and righteousness from the God of
    his salvation."

Speaking in his native Gaelic, the young man said, "Brethren, it seems to me just sentimental humbug to be praying as we are praying, to be waiting as we are waiting here, if we ourselves are not rightly related to God." Then he asked the Lord, "Are my hands clean, is my heart pure?"[1] He and his fellow intercessors fell on their faces in that barn, and their lives were revived as they got their hands and hearts clean before the Lord.

Duncan Campbell, an itinerant minister, was invited to lead a series of services in their town. By Sunday of the first week, the whole island was filled with a God-consciousness. Churches were filled to overflowing. Groups and crowds met in the fields and by the roadside to get right with God. Youth left a dance at midnight to go to church. People who couldn't sleep came to church in the middle of the night to get right with God. In one Scottish community not a home was left without someone coming to Christ.

Over the next four years God poured waters on the thirsty ground in keeping with His promise that those with clean hands and a pure heart would receive a downpour of blessing from the Lord. ✝

---

1. Duncan Campbell, *The Price and Power of Revival: Lessons from the Hebribes Awakening* (Vinton, VA: Christ Life Publications), 32.

sin in the mirror:
a picture of brokenness

PART 1

sin in the mirror:
a picture of brokenness

PART 1

key verse to memorize

*"The wrath of God is revealed from heaven against
all ungodliness and unrighteousness of men, who
by their unrighteousness suppress the truth."*
Romans 1:18

For session 4 plans, turn to page 170 in the leader guide.

discussion guide on week 3: God on the throne, part 2
1. What aspect of God's glory wows you the most (activity 2, p. 40)?
2. What is the book of life, and how would you know your name is written there (day 3)?
3. What meaningful or striking statements did you identify in Jonathan Edwards's sermon (activity 1, p. 45)?
4. Did you spend time with someone explaining what you have learned about holiness this week (activities 2 and 3, pp. 46-47)? If so, whom did you talk with, and how did they respond?
5. Use some of the questions in activity 3 on page 47 to review what you have learned during the study of God on the throne.
6. What did you learn from the revival in the Hebrides Islands of Scotland that can help you and your group know how to pray for personal revival?

dvd session 4 message notes (38 minutes)
Scripture focus: Romans 1:18-20
1. Sin brings God's _____ (Rom. 1:18a).
   A. Origin of Sin (Gen. 2:16; Gen. 3:6; Rom. 5:12; Ps. 51:5; Rom. 5:10; Col. 1:21; Jas. 4:4; Eph. 2:3; John 3:36;)
   B. Extent of Sin (1 John 1:8; Rom. 3:23; Eccl. 7:20; Rom. 7:18-19; 1 Tim. 5:24)
   C. Intent of Sin. Sin will pursue you (Gen. 4:7), disappoint you (Heb. 11:25), trip you up (Heb. 12:1), enslave you (Rom. 6:16), and expose you (Prov. 28:13; Num. 32:23).
2. Sin is _____ (Rom. 1:18-20).
   A. I _____ from the truth (Rom. 1:18b). I am responsible.

downpour

snapshot summary

Sin left unchecked has devastating results, but God works to reveal our sin to us so that we can turn away from sin and back to Him.

my goals for you

I want you to understand the destructive nature of sin and demonstrate your determination to see your sin in the mirror.

B. My _____ convicts me (Rom. 1:19). I cannot plead ignorance.

C. My _____ convicts me (Rom. 1:20). I have no excuse.

Testimony: Andi's impurity, discipline, and restoration. "Remember, the grace of God is big enough to cover this."

responding to the message

1. Review by answering the following questions.
   a. Which of the following definitions of *sin* helps you best understand the concept?
      • Sin is any failure to conform to God's law in action, in failure to act, or in attitude.
      • Sin: to miss the mark
      • Sin: choosing what God forbids or refusing what God demands
      • Sin: leaving the good undone (see Jas. 4:17).
   b. Which Scripture about sin's extent and/or intent was the most sobering?
   c. What did you learn from Andi's testimony about the consequences of sin?
2. Pray that God will help you and all your group see sin in the mirror so that you may deal with it in repentance.

preview statements for this week's study

• We're desperately riddled with the cancer of sin. Unless we embrace an aggressive treatment plan, it's terminal.
• Sin is any failure to conform to God's standard from His Word—in action, in failure to act, or in attitude.
• God would rather have the meaningful worship of a few rather than the robotic worship of the masses.

Message-notes blanks: wrath, inexcusable, turn, conscience, Creator

day 1 | Taking Sin Seriously

Does anybody like going to the doctor? No, but we do it because we know that if we have a problem, we need it diagnosed, treated, and out of our lives. What good would it do if the doctor saw a big, dark spot on our X-ray and sent us home, telling us everything was fine? The doctor might rationalize, *Oh, I wanted to tell them the truth, but I knew it would ruin their day.*

❶ If you went to the doctor and he discovered you had aggressive cancer, what information would you want from him? Check one.
  ❏ a. I'd want the whole truth about my cancer, the treatment options, and the prospects for recovery.
  ❏ b. I'd want him to sugarcoat the truth so that I wouldn't feel bad about my condition.
  ❏ c. I'd want him to lie to me and tell me everything is OK.

In some ways a correct diagnosis is a relief, no matter how serious the prognosis. I doubt you've ever heard anyone say, "What's a little cancer? Let it go." Now we know what we need to go after. "Do the surgery, Doc. Get it all!" Only the most foolish would choose the lie rather than the truth.

Last week we visited the throne room of heaven and got a fresh view of the holy, exalted God of the universe. Understanding holiness and God's incredibly high standards for human behavior makes His command for us to "be holy, for I am holy" (1 Pet. 1:16) totally overwhelming. It reveals to us how pitifully ravaged we are by sin and what our lives have become. There's no way any of us could compare ourselves to God's holy stature. We're desperately riddled with the cancer of sin. Unless we embrace an aggressive treatment plan, it's terminal.

"Wait a minute," you say. "I'm a Christian! Jesus forgave my sins." Yes, He did. Christ paid the full price for your redemption. Through faith in Him your salvation is secure. That's the eternal picture, but don't make the mistake so many Christians do by confusing salvation with sanctification. The former deals with your eternal standing before God in Christ; the latter deals with God's postconversion work in you today. What are you allowing God to do about sin in your life today? Even though you have been forgiven and saved by the work of Jesus Christ, there remains in you a definite bent toward doing things your own way. God wants sin out of your life because it's the only thing that keeps you from experiencing the torrential downpour of blessing He wants to rain on you.

❷ Match the word on the left with the correct description on the right. Write a letter beside the number.
  ___ 1. salvation   a. Growing in Christlikeness and becoming increasingly free from choosing to sin
  ___ 2. sanctification b. Receiving Christ's eternal forgiveness for my sin

(Answers: 1-b, 2-a)

We have learned in Hosea 6 about God's readiness to open the windows of heaven and pour down His blessing on the parched ground of our hearts. We know that will happen only when we return to Him. Returning begins by seeing the sin in your life for what it is—a barrier between you and fellowship with a holy God.

Drop the Umbrella ☂

Sin is like an umbrella. God's grace can be pouring down all around you, even blessing your family or friends at church, but all God is giving fails to fall on you because of sin. Like a big umbrella held high over your head, sin blocks the showers of blessing from reaching your life.

You can study the Bible until your head explodes or serve in Sunday School until the church wants to hire you full-time; but in the end your relationship with God is about just one thing: putting away your sin. If you are not dealing with it as God prescribes, your spiritual arteries will be clogged, and no amount of study or service will get the blood pumping consistently. That's the bottom line. You have to deal with sin God's way.

It's *your* sin that hinders you from experiencing a downpour of revival. Not sin in the neighborhood, not sin in the newspaper but sin in the mirror. Sin is the answer to questions like: *Why don't I feel close to God the way I used to? What happened to my passion for God?* Sin is what's in the way.

For the most part, evangelical Christians are good at seeing sin on television and in the church lobby, but we miserably fail at seeing sin in the mirror. "The heart is deceitful above all things, and desperately sick; who can understand it?" (Jer. 17:9). Our capacity to deceive ourselves leads us to believe we are holier than we really are. Our sinful hearts trick us into thinking that *everyone else has problems, but not me.* As one preacher rightly asserts, "You're being lied to, and it's an inside job." It's your own heart that lies to you about personal sin—and that deception is death to downpour.

If we don't see the horror of sin and God's holy intensity about sin, we'll never be able to rightly comprehend or understand why it needs to be taken so seriously. Sin brings God's wrath. Romans 1:18 says, "The wrath of God is revealed from heaven against all ungodliness and unrighteousness of men, who by their unrighteousness suppress the truth."

❸ Based on Romans 1:18, what and who are the objects of God's wrath?

_____

_____

Tell God you realize that you can deceive yourself about your sin. Ask Him to show you the sin in your life that hinders your sense of His presence and the downpour of His blessing. Agree with Him that you will throw away every "umbrella" (sin barrier) He reveals. ☂

Sin's Origin, Extent, and Intent

After the glory of Jesus Christ, who is the solution to sin, the next most dominant theme in Scripture is sin itself. More than two thousand times the Bible uses various synonyms to refer to sin, ungodliness, wickedness, or unrighteousness. On nearly every page and in nearly every chapter, this destructive human condition is described in horrific detail.

Sin Defined

Sin is any failure to conform to God's standard from His Word—in action, in failure to act, or in attitude. The Hebrew word is *chata'*; the Greek word is *hamartia*. Both of these words mean *to miss the mark,* as in an archer's target, but of course, God doesn't play games. Sin is much more serious than "Oops, I didn't get a bull's-eye." Or "Uh-oh, missed again; I really stink at this." No, sin is not a game. It's the reason for every dark human experience. It's the reason Christ's death was necessary. Romans 6:23 says, "The wages of sin is death."

❶ **See if you can identify the words or phrases that are related to sin. Check all that apply.**

❏ righteousness	❏ transgression	❏ missing the mark
❏ iniquity	❏ unrighteousness	❏ evil
❏ trespass	❏ lawless	❏ disobedience
❏ ungodly	❏ unholy	❏ misdeed
❏ wrong	❏ wickedness	❏ rebellion

If you checked all but *righteousness*, you are correct. Where does all this sin come from?

The Origin of Our Sin

Many of the problems, struggles, and fears you face today are because of what happened in the garden of Eden in the very first days of history. Adam and Eve chose to go their own way. In Genesis 2:16-17 God told them, "You may surely eat of every tree of the garden, but of the tree of the knowledge of good and evil you shall not eat, for in the day that you eat of it you shall surely die." They were created with the freedom to choose, and they chose the only thing God forbade. According to Genesis 3:6-7, "When the woman saw that the tree was good for food, and that it was a delight to the eyes, and that the tree was to be desired to make one wise, she took of its fruit and ate; and she also gave some to her husband who was with her, and he ate. Then the eyes of both were opened, and they knew that they were naked." They surrendered their innocence to sin.

The Bible teaches that Adam and Eve passed their sin nature, like a bad gene, to all of humankind. Romans 5:12,19 reports, "Just as sin came into the world through one man, and death through sin, and so death spread to all men ... by the one man's disobedience the many were made sinners." David said in Psalm 51:5, "Behold, I was brought forth in iniquity, / and in sin did

downpour

my mother conceive me." Apart from God's grace, the intent of our heart is "only evil continually" (Gen. 6:5).

As harsh as it sounds, that makes every unbeliever an enemy of God. We do not have to do anything to become God's enemies; we are born that way (see Rom. 5:10; Col. 1:21; Jas. 4:4). The New Testament refers to those without Christ as "children of wrath" (Eph. 2:3; also see John 3:36). Every person born into this world is born with an inclination to sin.

The Extent of Our Sin

Just how far does this sin nature reach? (Hint: to the core.)

1. Everybody is a sinner. Ecclesiastes 7:20 says, "Surely there is not a righteous man on earth who does good and never sins." Romans 3:23 echoes, "All have sinned and fall short of the glory of God."

2. To claim otherwise is self-deceit. First John 1:8, 10 teaches, "If we say we have no sin, we deceive ourselves, and the truth is not in us. ... If we say we have not sinned, we make him a liar, and his word is not in us."

3. Even the apostles acknowledged sin. The Apostle Paul writes in Romans 7:18, "I know that nothing good dwells in me, that is, in my flesh. For I have the desire to do what is right, but not the ability to carry it out."

4. Even those who are not obviously sinful are still sinners. First Timothy 5:24 testifies, "The sins of some men are conspicuous, going before them to judgment, but the sins of others appear later."

❷ Mark the following statements *T* for *true* or *F* for *false.*

___ 1. God created Adam and Eve sinful. They didn't have to do anything to become sinners.
___ 2. Sin entered the world by the disobedience of one man.
___ 3. All persons are sinners by birth and by personal choice.
___ 4. Only a few of the apostles lived without sin.
___ 5. If a person says she has not sinned, she is self-deceived.
___ 6. The sin of some is more obvious than the sin of others.

(Answers: T–2, 3, 5, 6; F–1, 4)

OK. So we've *all* got a sin problem. Yes, and it's a slippery slope. Let's continue our study of the most common subject of Scripture with a look at where sin takes us.

The Intent of Sin

1. Sin will pursue you. Before Cain murdered his brother, Abel, God told him, "If you do not do well, sin is crouching at the door. Its desire is for you, but you must rule over it." Cain did not heed the warning, and sin pursued and conquered him (see Gen. 4:7,11-12).

2. Sin will disappoint you. Hebrews 11:25 says that the pleasures of sin are only for a season. Time will run out, and misery will be waiting on the other side. Sin will always disappoint you; don't allow yourself to believe otherwise.

3. Sin will trip you up. Hebrews 12:1 says, "Let us lay aside every weight, and the sin which so easily ensnares us" (NKJV). You're going along doing pretty well, and suddenly you're flat on your face. Satan will spot your weakness and set sin under your feet. If you don't lay aside the opportunity to sin, you will eventually, inevitably crash. Sin trips you up.

4. Sin will enslave you. Paul tells us in Romans 6:16 that sin is addictive: "Do you not know that if you present yourselves to anyone as obedient slaves, you are slaves of the one whom you obey, either of sin, which leads to death, or of obedience, which leads to righteousness?" You are the slave of the one you obey. When sin whispers in your ear, "Do it, do it, do it," and you lean in to listen, you are on the pathway to addiction.

5. Sin will expose you. Don't be fooled. Proverbs 28:13 says, "Whoever conceals his transgressions will not prosper." Numbers 32:23 affirms, "Be sure your sin will find you out." If you're sitting on a secret as you read this book, news flash! It's coming out! You had better deal with it soon. Yes, it's embarrassing but all the worse if someone must force you to see it.

③ How thoroughly has sin done its work on you? Check each way you have experienced consequences of sin.
- ❏ a. I've been pursued by sin. It crouched at my door.
- ❏ b. Sin promised pleasure, but in the end it disappointed me.
- ❏ c. I got tripped up by sin. Ensnared? Yes.
- ❏ d. I have experienced an addiction to sin. It was my master.
- ❏ e. I have been caught and exposed by sin. How embarrassing!

Sin will pursue you, disappoint you, trip you up, enslave you, and ultimately expose you. No wonder sin brings God's wrath. If you are feeling beaten down at the moment, let me remind you there is hope. We're headed to forgiveness, victory, and freedom over sin.

Spend some time before the Lord and remember all of the times and ways your life has been hurt by the consequences of sin. Tell Him how sick and tired you are of sin and its effects. Name to Him the ways you want to be set free from the guilt, bondage, and influence of sin. Ask Him to guide you all the way out. ✝

day 3 | Why Is the World So Messed Up?

Romans 1:18 says, "The wrath of God is revealed from heaven against all ungodliness and unrighteousness." That term *ungodliness* means *to disrespect faith, to think lowly of all things that are spiritual.* Unrighteousness is the idea of pushing aside what is right. The wrath of God—God's deep-seated, burning, holy anger against sin—is revealed from heaven.

Something inside each of us demands and calls out for justice. If we see a wrong being done, like someone stealing a woman's purse or breaking in line at the bank or trying to hurt an innocent person, most of us feel a surge of anger rising within us. This is true because we are made in God's image. Even though our hearts are sinful and selfish, we feel righteous anger toward the wrong done. How much greater, then, is the anger of an infinitely holy God when we choose to break His law? The verb tense of the word *revealed* (in the original Greek) carries the idea of ongoing action. God's wrath is continually being revealed in our world today. It's happening right now.

You cannot explain the injustice and heartache that are broadcast on every form of media from every corner of the world without a proper theology of sin. You cannot explain what God allows, promotes, and causes in this world if you don't comprehend the holiness of God and the wrath of God that is directed against sin. And if you understand what Scripture says about the end times, then you know that as far as God's wrath is concerned, we "ain't seen nothing yet." It's how holiness feels about sin. Sin brings God's wrath.

❶ Look back at Romans 1:18 at the beginning of today's lesson. What brings God's wrath?

_____ and _____

No Excuses

Ungodliness and unrighteousness bring God's wrath. I don't know about you, but all this talk about sin is making me feel kinda sick. Can't we move on to the solution? Not yet. Not until this theology of sin invades our own lives. *But my sin isn't hurting anyone. How could it be so wrong when it feels so right? It's not like I'm the only one ever to struggle with this.*

The universality of our rationalizations reveals the commonality of our struggle. Each of us has little phrases we repeat to ourselves when we feel the slightest touch of conviction. Wake up! Don't be deceived. Downpour is only a pipe dream until you admit that God's primary interest is not your skill in diagnosing the sin of others. He wants to get *you* into surgery. God has freed you from the penalty of sin for all eternity through your faith in Jesus. Now God wants to go after the power of sin in your life here and now. Romans 6:14 says, "Sin will have no dominion over you, since you are not under law but under grace."

Why Won't God Just Eliminate Sin?

Some people argue that if God didn't want sin in the world, He should have made a world where there was no sin. Oh sure, He could have made us robots. Instead, God made a world in which we have the freedom to choose, knowing that many would reject Him and a few would choose to give their affections in worship to the One who made it all. God would rather have the meaning-ful worship of a few rather than the robotic worship of the masses. Nobody wants coerced affection, least of all God. Genuine worship and love from the souls of a few—that's the choice God made.

Because God created a world in which we are free to choose, I am respon-sible for my own sinful choices. Romans 1:18 makes it clear that no one chooses my sin but me: "... who by their unrighteousness suppress the truth." That word *suppress* means *to hold down*. Sin stiff-arms and squelches God. Sin suppresses the flow of God's favor toward me. Every choice to do wrong, every choice to leave good undone, every wrong attitude perpetuated and promoted in my life is a choice to push God away—and it's called sin.

② Mark the following statements *T* for *true* or *F* for *false*.

___ 1. God created me to be sinful, so I really don't have a choice about sin.
___ 2. God created me free to choose love and obedience or sin. I have a choice.
___ 3. God prefers the coerced love of the masses' robotic worship.
___ 4. God prefers the sincere worship of those who choose to love Him.

(Answers: T–2, 4; F–1, 3)

Sin Suppresses the Fact of God's Existence

You may have heard about the boy who stood holding a string that went up into the clouds. A passerby asked him, "What are you doing?"

"I'm flying a kite," the boy said.

"Well, how do you know? You can't see the kite."

"Well, every so often I feel the tug on the string."

It's like that with God, isn't it? I've never seen God, but I feel the tug on the string. That's the God-consciousness in each of us.

According to the 2006 Barna research, 71 percent of people admit they believe there is a God.[1] Why? Because it's in our hearts. Think of the most evil, dastardly person of whom you've ever heard. Deep within that person's heart is a suppressed awareness of God's existence. It's there in all of us. Maybe science will one day discover the "God gene," but either way this inherent knowledge of God's existence is there because God put it there. Ecclesiastes 3:11 states that God has "put eternity into man's heart." Theologians call this God-consciousness.

③ As a visual reminder of your God-consciousness, draw a kite on the end of a string. Include yourself in the picture.

You've got to work hard to suppress that sense of "Somebody's there. He sees me right now. He's keeping track." Do you have a sense of that? God put that in you. When you get away from God and embrace a life of sin, you hold that God-consciousness down. The truth is suppressed in unrighteousness. When you choose a life of sin, you suppress that inherent knowledge; you push it down.

Confess to the Lord your sorrow for all of the times you've suppressed the truth about Him. Invite Him to increase the tug on your kite string. ✝

1. "Beliefs: General Religious," *The Barna Group* [online, cited 03 July 2006]. Available from the Internet: *www.barna.org/FlexPage.aspx?Page = Topic&TopicID = 2*

day 4 | Sin Is My Choice

My Conscience Accuses Me

Beyond your heart knowledge of God, God has given to each of us a conscience—an internal alarm about what's right and wrong. Everyone is born with a conscience. None of us can plead ignorance. We can't show up in heaven someday and say, "Oh, I'm so sorry, God. I didn't know." Romans 1:19 says, "What can be known about God is plain to them, because God has shown it to them." I love that. What can be known about God is clearly seen. It's evident to us because God has woven it into our conscience. God made you to know some things about Him. He wrote them on our hearts.

Look at Romans 2:14-15: "When Gentiles, who do not have the law, by nature do what the law requires, they are a law to themselves, even though they do not have the law. They show that the work of the law is *written on their hearts,* while their conscience also bears witness, and their conflicting thoughts accuse or even excuse them" (emphasis added). That's conscience.

Can you let your conscience be your guide? No, you cannot. First, your conscience is conditioned by what you know. The more you stay in God's Word, the more tender your conscience grows. Second, your conscience is conditioned by what you do. The more you do right, the more tenderhearted you become. The more you do wrong, the more calloused and hard you become. That's why 1 Timothy 4:2 says your conscience can actually become seared or lose its capacity to feel pain. If you feel no twinge of guilt about sin, it's because your conscience has been seared. Eventually, some people become pathological and criminally evil because they silenced their conscience through repeated sin.

❶ Match the conscience on the right with the things that develop or result from such a conscience on the left. Write a letter beside each number.

___ 1. No feelings of guilt about sin   a. Tender, sensitive conscience
___ 2. Produced by repeated sin   b. Calloused, seared conscience
___ 3. Developed by doing right
___ 4. Developed by spending time in God's Word

(Answers: 1–b, 2–b, 3–a, 4–a)

My Creator Convicts Me

Not only does my conscience convict me, but God Himself also convicts me that I will answer for the choices I make. Romans 1:20 says, "His invisible attributes, namely, his eternal power and divine nature, have been clearly perceived, ever since the creation of the world, in the things that have been made. So they are without excuse."

I was playing golf with a couple of guys this week who are a lot better golfers than I am. I wasn't hitting the ball very well—sometimes it went left, sometimes right. I think I need new clubs. But honestly, it's not the tools; it's the tradesman. The problem isn't the golf club; the problem is the golfer. It's the law of cause and effect. It's a basic law of the universe. The idea of an effect without a cause is the height of foolishness.

A high fever left 19-month-old Helen Keller without sight, hearing, and speech. But from age seven, she was blessed to have an excellent teacher in

Anne Sullivan. Anne taught Helen how to communicate through touch. As they began to communicate, one of the first things Anne introduced to Helen was God. Young Helen said in sign language, "I already knew there was a God. I just didn't know His name."

"The fool says in his heart, 'There is no God' " (Ps. 14:1). Creation shouts God's existence. To say that creation was self-originating contradicts the law of cause and effect. Evolution is one of the greatest lies Satan has raised on the flagpole of human understanding. The reason so many people cling with such tenacity to a theory that is very bad science is because they're suppressing the truth in unrighteousness.

Do you remember when Jonah was running from God (see Jonah 1)? The sailors on the boat, frantic because of the storm, came to Jonah with these words: "You better start praying to your God, Man." Jonah confessed, "I worship the God of heaven and earth." And the sailors were like, "Oh. That God." They all knew. After Jonah went into the fish, they had a worship service. We may see that whole crew in heaven someday.

Paul stood on the rocky hill that served as the sacred meeting place of the Athenian prime council. Read his argument for God's existence:

> *"Men of Athens, I perceive that in every way you are very religious. For as I passed along and observed the objects of your worship, I found also an altar with this inscription, 'To the unknown god.' What therefore you worship as unknown, this I proclaim to you. The God who made the world and everything in it, being Lord of heaven and earth, does not live in temples made by man, nor is he served by human hands, as though he needed anything, since he himself gives to all mankind life and breath and everything. And he made from one man every nation of mankind to live on all the face of the earth, having determined allotted periods and the boundaries of their dwelling place, that they should seek God, in the hope that they might feel their way toward him and find him. Yet he is actually not far from each one of us, for 'In him we live and move and have our being'; as even some of your own poets have said, 'For we are indeed his offspring.' "*
>
> **Acts 17:22-28**

Romans 1 says that at the height of our sinful nature, we suppress the reality of God's existence. Verse 20 says that we are "without excuse." Literally, we have no defense. Have you ever pressed for a reason from a person who says he doesn't believe in God? He has no defense. Sin wants it to be true. Sin is shouting, "Ignore the truth, ignore your conscience, ignore the Creator!" God has given every person a chance to know the truth. We have no excuse.

❱ **Pray that God will continue to make His existence real to you. Pray that you will have opportunities to testify to others of His reality.** ↑

day 5 | David's Personal Revival

❶ In 2 Samuel 11 we read about David's sins of adultery and murder. Read 2 Samuel 12:1-25 in your Bible and answer these questions.

1. How had God blessed David prior to this sin (vv. 7-8)?

_____

_____

2. With what sins did Nathan confront David (v. 9)?

_____

3. What would the consequences for David's sin be?

Verse 10: _____

Verses 11-12: _____

Verse 13: _____

4. Since the baby had already been born to Bathsheba, how long had David been covering up his sin before Nathan confronted him?
   ❏ a. Just a few days
   ❏ b. At least nine months

5. After David's repentance God gave him and Bathsheba another son. What did Bathsheba name him? _____

6. God sent another name for him through the prophet Nathan. What was that name? _____ (which means *Beloved of the LORD*)

❷ Now read on page 62 about the picture of personal revival from David's life. Underline key ideas from Psalm 51 that give you examples for a prayer of repentance.

❸ Read about the joy of forgiveness in David's Psalm 32. Underline verses you would like to memorize.

❹ Use Psalm 51 as a model for a prayer of your own. Read it as a prayer and make personal application to your own life.

From the Life of David: A Picture of Brokenness

2 SAMUEL 12; PSALM 51

How did I end up over here? King David probably wondered that as he put down the mirror that Nathan had held in front of him. His entire life had been marked by a faith and trust that burned hot for God. *Who was this prodigal in the mirror?*

How many times had David cried out for God in the crucible and God had refined him like gold? How many private conversations had he had with the Lover of his soul on the slopes of Bethlehem, tending sheep? In the caves of En Gedi while running from Saul? Coming home from battle with the songs of triumph ringing in his ears? *How long has it been since I've known that spiritual victory? Since I've felt that close to God? What happened to the joy of my salvation?*

That's what Nathan had come to help David answer. Somewhere along the way, David's compromises, the lost priorities, the increasing distance from God had slowly dried up his heart. Sin had done what sin always does. And the best worship leader in the history of Israel had been quieted.

David now knew what needed to be done, and it was something only God could accomplish. David needed new life breathed into his spirit. He needed a downpour of forgiveness to wash over his dry and thirsty soul.

For the first time in a long time, David understood that the path to revival began with his turning around. Psalm 51 records his willingness:

"Have mercy on me, O God." Deal with this sin in my life, Lord. I come on Your terms.

"My sin is ever before me." What I have ignored, dismissed, and rationalized is now staring me in the face. It's my sin. It's my fault.

"Against you, you only, have I sinned." You are a righteous and holy God. This sin has hurt Your name. I've caused others to misunderstand Your holiness.

"Create in me a clean heart, O God." Do the surgery, Lord. Get it all.

"The sacrifices of God are ... a broken and contrite heart." The one thing You require is the only thing I can offer, Lord. Here I am—shattered by my sin and what it has cost You. Please make me whole again.

"Renew a right spirit within me." Help me stay in this place until Your work is complete. Please make my heart alive again.

"Restore to me the joy of your salvation." Revive me, Lord.

And God did bring revival to David's soul—as God promises to do for every broken heart that comes to Him in humility and faith. ✝

sin in the mirror:
a picture of brokenness

sin in the mirror: a picture of brokenness

PART 2

key verse to memorize

"Confess your sins to one another and pray for one another, that you may be healed. The prayer of a righteous person has great power as it is working."

James 5:16

For session 5 plans, turn to page 171 in the leader guide.

discussion guide on week 4: sin in the mirror, part 1

1. What is the difference between forgiveness for salvation and forgiveness in sanctification (day 1)?
2. How would you define the word *sin?* What are some synonyms (p. 54)?
3. Review the true/false statements in activity 2 on page 55.
4. What are five things sin will do to you if given the opportunity? (See "The Intent of Sin" on pp. 55–56.)
5. Why doesn't God eliminate sin (p. 57)?
6. Describe how you can develop a tender conscience and a calloused one.
7. Using David's example (pp. 61–62), answer this question: Can a person be forgiven and still have to suffer the consequences of sin?

dvd session 5 message notes (34 minutes)

Scripture focus: Romans 1:21-32

3. Sin has a _____ (Rom. 1:21).
    A. _____ to honor God (Rom. 1:21a)
    B. _____ thinking (Rom. 1:21b)
    C. _____ religion (Rom. 1:22-23)
4. Sin only _____ (Rom. 1:24-32).
    A. Unrestrained _____ (Rom. 1:24)
    B. Leads to _____ (Rom. 1:26-27)
    C. Leads to _____ (Rom. 1:28-31)
    D. Leads to _____ of same (Rom. 1:32)
5. Sin in the mirror: it's not too late to _____ (vv. 23,25-26,28)
    See the list of sins on page 67.

 Message music: see the "Good and Faithful Friend" lyrics on page 66.

snapshot summary

Sin's pattern is to escalate your turning away from God. Don't let it go on one more day. Today, if you hear His voice … turn around!

my goals for you

I want you to understand the consequences of sin, and I want you to show your brokenness over sin by turning back to the Lord.

responding to the message

1. Review the lyrics to "Good and Faithful Friend" and read the last verse in unison. This is why we're dealing with sin in the mirror—to get to the victory side where the power of sin is gone. Ask a volunteer to pray that God will provide grace to complete the hard work of dealing seriously with sin.
2. In same-gender groups of three (men with men, women with women):
   a. Read James 5:16.
   b. Complete together the first message-music activity on page 66. Candidly share your needs for God's work of grace in setting you free from sin.
   c. Take time to pray for one another, one person at a time. Pray specifically for cleansing, forgiveness, and deliverance from the power of sin. You may want to ask, *How may we pray for you?* Then pray.
   d. Discuss a possible time or way the three of you can get together again before the next small-group session to "confess your sins to one another and pray for one another." Consider a time during the next week, meeting early before the next session, a conference call, or other options for helping one another move on to victory. See day 3 for more directions.

preview statements for this week's study

- Nobody sees personal sin from "high on their horse." We have to get low to recognize the way sin is clogging the arteries of our relationship with God.
- Your increased sensitivity to sin is a mark of a heart that God is reviving.
- James 5:16 says, "Confess your sins to one another and pray for one another, that you may be healed. The prayer of a righteous person has great power as it is working." That's what we are going after—healing, righteousness, and power in prayer.

Message-notes blanks: pattern, Failure, Futile, Foolish, escalates, passion, perversion, pandemonium, promotion, turn

Good and Faithful Friend

it's time to make a change / and turn my life around
press on toward the blood stained cross / where purity is found
You lift me from the mire / into the whitest snow
how can it be with all my sin / a King would lead me home

though I keep falling,
You still keep calling out my name
then embrace me once again
what a good and faithful friend
i know You're grieving
and that's why I'm leaving sin behind
for the grace I'll always find
from my good and faithful friend

Lord, open up my eyes / to see what You have seen
i ask for Your forgiveness where / forgiveness has not been
so rejoice my soul, rejoice / the power of sin has gone
Your mercy brought me to this place / and Your grace will lead me on

———

*"I waited patiently for the Lord; / he inclined to me and heard my cry.
He drew me up from the pit of destruction, / out of the miry bog,
and set my feet upon a rock, / making my steps secure.
He put a new song in my mouth, / a song of praise to our God."*

Psalm 40:1-3

**Slowly read the lyrics above and meditate on the meaning of this song.
Use the following questions to better grasp God's goodness to you.**

1. What actions described in the song are the activities of God as a good and faithful Friend? Underline them.
2. What, if any, are reasons in your life that "it's time to make a change"?
3. How would "I keep falling" describe a time or problem in your life?

This week listen to the song on your Message-Music CD (track 3) and listen to the Lord calling your name. Let Him embrace you.

Confess to the Lord unconfessed sin that comes to your mind and leave it behind. Use the lyrics to express your desire for the Lord's work in your life and let your soul rejoice at the forgiveness He provides.

| # Getting Specific with Sin*

____ Addiction
____ Anger
____ Bigotry
____ Boastful
____ Causing dissension
____ Controlled by emotions
____ Covetousness
____ Deceitfulness
____ Dishonesty
____ Domineering
____ Drunkenness
____ False guilt
____ False witness
____ Feeling helpless
____ Feeling stupid
____ Gluttony
____ Greediness
____ Homosexual lust
____ Idolatry
____ Impulsiveness
____ Indifferent to needs
____ Insecurity
____ Jealousy
____ Loner
____ Lust for pleasure
____ Materialistic
____ Must repay kindness
____ Occult involvement
____ Oppressive
____ Overly sensitive to criticism
____ Prejudice
____ Profanity
____ Rebellion to authority
____ Resentment
____ Sadness (anxiety)
____ Self-confidence
____ Self-hatred
____ Self-justification
____ Self-reliance
____ Self-sufficiency
____ Sexual immorality
____ Slander
____ Temper
____ Unjust
____ Vanity

____ Adultery
____ Argumentative
____ Bitterness
____ Bossiness
____ Conceit
____ Controlled by peer pressure
____ Critical tongue
____ Depression
____ Disrespectful
____ Drug dependency
____ Envy
____ False modesty
____ Fear
____ Feeling rejected
____ Feeling worthless
____ Gossip
____ Hatred
____ Hostility
____ Impatience
____ Impure thoughts
____ Inhibited
____ Intemperance
____ Laziness
____ Low self-esteem
____ Lying
____ Murder
____ Negativism
____ Opinionated
____ Overly quiet
____ Passivity
____ Pride
____ Projecting blame
____ Refuse to forgive
____ Restlessness
____ Self-centeredness
____ Self-gratification
____ Self-indulgence
____ Self-pity
____ Self-righteousness
____ Sensuality
____ Sexual lust
____ Stubbornness
____ Theft
____ Unloving
____ Workaholic

*See instructions on page 68.

It's Not Too Late to Turn

We've looked at God on the throne, a picture of holiness. We discussed the importance of seeing God in His rightful place, high and lifted up. Only when we see God and His infinite standard of holiness do we begin to open our hearts to the reality of how far short all of us fall (see Rom. 3:23).

The purpose of this week's study is to help us get low enough to see sin in the mirror. Nobody sees personal sin from "high on their horse." We have to get low to recognize the way sin is clogging the arteries of our relationship with God. We need to give God unlimited access, full permission to shine His light into every dark corner of our souls.

Do the surgery, God. Get it all.

Pray as you pull out your "mirror" and ask God to show you what is keeping your life dry and distant from Him. Pray: *I want this cancer of sin removed, and I know that must begin with an accurate diagnosis. Show me my sin as You see it and be as specific as You need to be. Help me be honest with myself and before You.*

Activate

This activity may take you more than one day to complete. I'm allowing two days for this lesson to give you more time. Take the time you need. Spread it out over a couple of days if necessary. Review it during the week and allow God to continue His working in your heart and mind.

1 **Sin is both attitude and action. On page 67 is a list of sins that believers deal with every day. Place a number from 0 to 10 beside each item to indicate the extent of its presence in your life. Mark 0 if it is not an issue at all and 10 if it is a point of frequent failure in your life. Go slowly, asking God for total honesty and a refusal to play games or pretend anymore. Focus on the sins you have not already dealt with before God. If you have already repented of a sin and are walking in victory, you don't need to deal with it again unless it has resurfaced.**

2 **In a journal or a notebook list sins about which God is bringing conviction. Make two columns. In the left column describe the sin very specifically. In the right column describe the consequences. What is the result of this specific sin in you? In others? Add as many rows to your chart as you need. One example is given below.**

My Sin	My Consequences
A critical tongue. "I speak critically and harshly to my husband when he doesn't measure up to what I think he should; I want to hurt him with my words."	*Our relationship stinks.* "My husband is distant and preoccupied with other things. He hasn't paid attention to me in months."

This is a very hard exercise, but you can't go on until you've completed it. You may need to return to this list several times before you have complete honesty before God on all points. Keep in mind that your "bigger" sins are the things that hang over your life like an umbrella, deflecting God's blessing. I have faith that you are really ready to deal with these things God's way. That's coming next week, but there is no point scouring your heart if you avoid the difficult corners.

③ Go back over the list on page 67 and ask God to reveal to you any self-deception that may cloud your capacity to see your true self in the mirror. If you want to make absolutely sure, go over the list in a prayerful way with a trusted friend. If you are blessed to have such a friend, he or she can help you with spots where you may have blinded yourself to reality.

What Should I Do with This New Understanding of My Sin?

1. Are you newly aware of sins in your life that you didn't recognize as sin before? As discouraging as this fresh exposure is, do you see how good it is? Your increased sensitivity to sin is a mark of a heart that God is reviving.

2. Feel the weight of your sin. Don't move too quickly to "fixing it." Be broken by it. Let the weight of your failure and its painful consequences in your life build genuine grief in you. Don't run from the pain of your sin.

3. You will be tempted to put this off for another day, but don't avoid this hard work. Don't be deceived into thinking that God will wait forever for you to get right with Him. Have you entertained the idea that "I'm not ready yet to deal with this stuff? I'll come back to God when I'm in a better place"? That's foolish thinking. Hebrews 4:7 says, "Today, if you hear his voice, do not harden your hearts."

4. Don't go to bed tonight without doing this serious heart-work. Aren't you tired of carrying this burden around? Don't you want to be free of it? Don't you want all God has planned for you—a downpour?

5. Just do it! And you'll be ready for the downpour! The clouds are beginning to form even now.

Elevate

Lord, a few moments of honesty quickly bring my sin to mind. I see it. So do You. Let me see it in the same way You do—in all of its nastiness. I yield to You. I want a full understanding of the things that have kept my heart dry and at a distance from You. I see it all now—not just the "acceptable" sins, but the ones I've hidden and nurtured for years. Thank You for bringing them to light. I can't imagine my private life without this burden; but I'm here, right now in faith, asking that You take it all far away from me. No more covering. No more hiding. No more rationalizing. I believe You are stirring a revival within me, and I know this dealing with sin has to come first. So I am coming in faith that You will help me. In Jesus' name. Amen. ✝

Helping One Another

Replicate

James 5:16 says, "Confess your sins to one another and pray for one another, that you may be healed. The prayer of a righteous person has great power as it is working." That's what we are going after—healing, righteousness, and power in prayer. Some churches wrongly think you need to confess your sins to one person in a supposed position of superiority, but all Christians are on equal footing before God. We're a royal priesthood and a kingdom of priests (see 1 Pet. 2:9; Rev. 1:6). We can help one another in our relationships with God. There are two good reasons to confess to one another.

1. To get sin into the open. "If we walk in the light, [that is, get our sins out in the light where we can work on them] as he is in the light, we have fellowship with one another, and the blood of Jesus his Son cleanses us from all sin" (1 John 1:7).

❶ What is one reason to confess sins to one another and pray?

_____

2. To get prayer support. When someone who loves and supports you is aware of the sins that trip you up, he or she will become a faithful prayer supporter. Everyone wants to pray about things they know God is willing to do.

❷ What is a second reason to confess sins to one another and pray?

_____

Helping one another seek God's highest and best for our lives begins with this difficult step, but it continues in the joy of revival.

❸ Turn in your Bible and read 2 Corinthians 7:8-11. Underline phrases that describe what repentance produced in the Corinthian church.

❹ During your previous group session I recommended that you connect with a small group of men or women (your same gender). If you arranged to get together with that small group to help one another deal with your sin, follow your plan. Otherwise, meet with a brother or a sister in Christ very soon (men with men and women with women). Then practice James 5:16: "Confess your sins to one another and pray for one another." You don't need to go into detail about your sin. Don't try to rationalize or give reasons for your sin. No excuses. Don't try to justify your actions. Agree with God (confess) that you have sinned and ask for prayer to be set free.

Make every effort to complete this assignment prior to your next small-group session.

Pray that the Lord will enable you to humble yourself as you deal seriously with your sin. Ask Him to cleanse you thoroughly of sin and set you free from its power. Ask Him to help you minister to your brothers or sisters in Christ that they may also know His healing touch. ✝

day 4 | The Dangers of Unchecked Sin

In Romans 1:21 Paul wrote, "Although they knew God, they did not honor him as God or give thanks to him, but they became futile in their thinking, and their foolish hearts were darkened." Other words for *futile* are *foolish* or *pointless;* it's thinking that is soft or logically unsound. When sin drives decisions, we can expect a lot of foolish thinking. In fact, sin so distorts our discernment that we begin to think we can invent a god that will agree with us. Romans 1:22-23 summarizes, "Claiming to be wise, they became fools, and exchanged the glory of the immortal God for images resembling mortal man and birds and animals and reptiles."

Everybody worships. If you don't worship the God of creation through His Son, Jesus Christ, then you worship something else. The world is full of man-made religions and self-appointed, self-made, or substitute gods. To the sound-minded person, making up your own god is so insane that it's silly; but to the mind darkened by sin, it's the natural next step. Notice in the following Scriptures the consequences of unchecked sin.

① **Read the following Scriptures and underline the phrase "God gave them up" each time it occurs.**
- "God gave them up in the lusts of their hearts" (Rom. 1:24).
- "God gave them up to dishonorable passions" (Rom. 1:26).
- "Since they did not see fit to acknowledge God, God gave them up" (Rom. 1:28).

Does God Really Give People Up to Sin?
Samson was a slave to sensual pleasure. Remember how Delilah tempted him with sexual sin to learn the secret of his strength? Finally, she shaved off his hair and called out the enemy. Samson met the Philistines at the door saying, " 'I will go out as at other times and shake myself free.' But he did not know that the LORD had left him" (Judg. 16:20).

In fact, the Lord had departed from the whole nation of Israel. In Judges 10 God had told them, "You have forsaken Me. ... Therefore I will deliver you no more. Go and cry out to the gods which you have chosen; let them deliver you in your time of distress" (Judg. 10:13-14, NKJV). Their futile minds had so deteriorated because of sin that they had made up idols to take God's place. And God was saying, in effect, "You think that's better than Me? You think that's going to meet your needs? Go have that, and we'll see if your idols satisfy your hearts."

2 Read below what God says in Proverbs 1:24-31. Underline what God does in response to our rebellion. I've underlined an example for you.

> *"Because I have called and you refused to listen, / have stretched out my hand and no one has heeded, / because you have ignored all my counsel / and would have none of my reproof, /* <u>*I also will laugh at your calamity;*</u> */ I will mock when terror strikes you, when terror strikes you like a storm / and your calamity comes like a whirlwind, / when distress and anguish come upon you. Then they will call upon me, but I will not answer; / they will seek me diligently but will not find me. / Because they hated knowledge / and did not choose the fear of the LORD, would have none of my counsel / and despised all my reproof, therefore they shall eat the fruit of their way, and have their fill of their own devices."*

Proverbs 1:24-31

3 Read back through this Scripture above and circle the things God says His people have done that bring these responses from Him. One would be "you refused to listen."

When you refuse to listen when God calls, you do not heed, you ignore His counsel and reproof, you hate knowledge and choose not to fear the Lord; then you suffer the consequences of your sin. God laughs at your calamity, mocks when terror strikes like a whirlwind, refuses to answer your prayers, and hides His presence from you. He gives you up to the consequences of your sin. These consequences of choosing sin after coming to faith are seldom preached on or talked about in this day of hypergrace, but they are experienced all too often.

4 Think about your own experiences. Do you think you may have experienced some of these consequences because of your actions?
❏ Yes ❏ No

Hosea 4:17 echoes the consequence of unchecked sin in a believer's life: "Ephraim [Israel] is joined to idols; leave him alone." That's what God says. How many people does God look at today and say, "So-and-so is joined to idols; leave him alone"?

Jesus said this same thing in Matthew 15:14 about the Pharisees: "Let them alone; they are blind guides. And if the blind lead the blind, both will fall into a pit." They were left alone to the consequences of the sin they had chosen. We'd like to think God will give us more time. But the idea that "I'll come back to God when I'm good and ready" is foolishness. Grace easily turns to hypergrace in a world that has lost its view of God's throne room and a biblical theology of sin.

If you have hesitated over seriously dealing with your sin, look at what Paul says about the path of unchecked sin in Romans 1. I want to make sure you have fully considered the consequences of lingering in sin. I want you to notice where sin takes a person. If you are in Christ, God would not allow you, nor would you desire, to go down this road. But many people who think they are in Christ finally prove that they are not by making these choices. Keep reading and refresh your thinking on just how slippery the slope of sin actually is. Consider these four steps down.

1. Unrestrained Passion: "I want it even if it's wrong."

Romans 1:24 says, "God gave them up in the lusts of their hearts to impurity, to the dishonoring of their bodies among themselves, because they exchanged the truth about God for a lie." That word *impurity* means "indecent acts that defile the body" and make the person unclean. "Dishonoring their body" describes anything for which we should be ashamed.

5 **What is one step down the slippery slope of sin?**

exchange the truth about God for a lie

2. Perversion: "I want the wrong even if it hurts me."

Sadly, that's not where it ends. Romans 1:26 says, "For this reason God gave them up to dishonorable passions. For their women exchanged natural relations for those that are contrary to nature." You don't have to be a biologist to figure out the miraculous way God made a man and a woman to come together in the confines of marriage in an intimacy that is mutually satisfying and easily accomplished. That expression of marital intimacy is the way God created sex to be. "The men likewise gave up natural relations with women and were consumed with passion for one another, men committing shameless acts with men and receiving in themselves the due penalty for their error" (v. 27). This describes an unstoppable, insatiable appetite for things that only shame, enslave, destroy, and blind us to the reality of God's design.

In the 1980s President Reagan ordered the attorney general's commission on pornography. James Dobson was part of that commission. The study concluded that something about sexual sin escalates in intensity so that the user needs more and more perversion to gain the same amount of arousal. Unrestrained passion in step 1 leads to perversion.

6 **When a person gives in to sin without restraint, where does he or she go from there? Check the correct answer, based on Romans 1:26-27.**
   ❑ a. Nowhere. You can stay shallow in sin as long as you please, and you can control your passions.
   ❑ b. Upward. After a little ungodly passion satisfies your cravings, you can get back to righteous living. So go ahead and get it out of your system.
   ☑ c. Downward. When you start feeding on ungodly passions, your appetite increases, and you can't seem to stop yourself short of perversion.

Did you want to check a or b? That's usually the way we think, isn't it? We think we can sin and control how much, or we think sinning now will get the desire out of our system so that we can get back to right living. That's not reality. Unchecked sin puts you on a slippery slope toward perversion (c).

3. Pandemonium: "I want it even if it hurts others."

Romans 1:28 says, "Since they did not see fit to acknowledge God, God gave them up to a debased mind to do what ought not to be done. They were filled with all manner of unrighteousness, evil, covetousness, malice. They are full of envy, murder, strife, deceit, maliciousness. They are gossips, slanderers, haters of God, insolent, haughty, boastful, inventors of evil, disobedient to parents, foolish, faithless, heartless, ruthless."

Sexual sin is only the first illustration of the way wrong choices spiral out of control. Paul now adds many other sins to that list that we often excuse or ignore. But these sins bring shame and lost mental capacity, and they move from passion (what I want when I want it) to perversion (even if it hurts me) to pandemonium (even if it hurts others). Do you see anything familiar in this list?

- Envy (wishing you had the position or prestige of another)
- Murder (hating someone else from your heart)
- Strife (causing and continuing relational conflict)
- Deceit (giving a wrong impression on purpose)
- Maliciousness (expending energy to injure others)
- Gossip and slander (words that wound and separate people)
- Insolence (rude and resolute in your refusal to be influenced)
- Haughty or boastful (proud)
- Disobedient to parents (how did that get on the list?)
- Foolish (lost capacity to discern what is wise and best)
- Faithless (unwilling to trust or even turn to God in tough times)
- Heartless (cold and calculating in your callousness)
- Ruthless (unfeeling in regard to the pain your actions cause others)

Whatever the sin God wants to show you in the mirror, whatever He wants out of the way so that He can bring a great revival to your heart—whatever that sin is—it follows that same downward spiral from passion (what I want when I want it) to perversion (even if it hurts me) to pandemonium (even if it hurts others). The final step down is a full-on commitment to promote my sin.

4. Promotion of Sin

Ever see a gay pride parade or watch in dismay as promoters of abortion rights zealously advance their right to sin? Ever wonder how a person gets to such an awful place of total-blackout blindness?

Romans 1:32 says, "Though they know God's decree that those who practice such things deserve to die, they not only do them but give approval to those who practice them." When a person reaches this level, there is little hope he will ever come back. This is absolute rock bottom. He is in the grip of sin. When a person reaches this level of desperation, it usually concludes with self-destruction. Sin is ruthless, and Satan is a devourer.

❼ Put the four steps down in order by numbering them from 1 to 4.

   ___ a. Perversion   ___ c. Promotion of sin

   ___ b. Unrestrained passion   ___ d. Pandemonium

(Answers: a–2, b–1, c–4, d–3)

downpour

Ask God to convict you of any time you have yielded to temptation and ended up on this slippery slope of sin. If you're on it now, it's time to turn. Confess your sin to the Lord and repent. If you are not on that slope now, ask God to be your alarm that sounds anytime you start down that path. ↑

Matt 1:21

day 5 | Personal Revival for the Derksen Brothers

❶ Read on page 76 about the picture of personal revival for the Derksen brothers in the Canadian revival. Pay attention to the way pride can lead to bitterness and separation. Also notice how a pastor and a deacon were able to assist through counsel and prayer to see a breakthrough.

❷ What were the benefits of confession, repentance, and forgiveness by these two brothers? Check all that apply.
  ❏ a. The brothers and their families were restored to right relationships.
  ❏ b. Their obedience encouraged others to do the hard work of confession and repentance to find the same joy and freedom.
  ❏ c. God used their testimony to spread the experience of personal revival to other churches and cities.
  ❏ d. God received glory by demonstrating what He can do to reconcile broken relationships.

Did you check them all? You're right!

❸ Do you have any broken relationships? Have you offended anyone from whom you need to seek forgiveness? Has anyone offended you whom you need to forgive? Write initials or names in the margin or on a separate sheet of paper.

If any relationships came to your mind, talk with the Lord about how you need to go about making them right. Ask Him if there are individuals who can help you as the pastor and the deacon helped Sam and Arnold.

Pray that God will receive glory by the changes He brings about in the lives of people in your group and church. If you know of people with broken relationships in your church body, pray that God will bring conviction and lead them to reconciliation. ↑

The Derksen Brothers and the Canadian Revival (1971)

"Sam and Arnold Derksen had been feuding for thirteen years. Although the brothers attended the same church, they had not spoken for two years. When Sam walked down one aisle of the church, his brother walked out the other, or vice versa. All their bitterness had erupted because of their mutual involvement in the music program of the church. They had different ideas, different tastes, and above all, a different evaluation of each other's ability. They were so adept at concealing their mutual hatred that many people did not even know the hostility existed.

"Sam believed reconciliation was hopeless. They had tried to patch up their differences before and failed. There was no reason to think that their bitterness could be resolved now. But God was at work.

"One night, following the evening service, Arnold went to the basement of the church with the pastor and a deacon. The three men suggested that Sam join them. He agreed to do so, since he was deeply convicted about his attitude. But when he asked Arnold to forgive him, the reply was icy, 'Well, it's about time!' Sam was disillusioned. The episode confirmed his suspicions that they could not be reunited.

"Rather than let the brothers go, the pastor and deacon prayed. A few moments later, God shattered Arnold's haughty spirit. He broke under the conviction of the Holy Spirit and confessed his sins, crying to God for mercy. A member sitting in the auditorium said that he could hear the men praying, crying, and beating on the downstairs wall. A few moments later, the brothers asked each other's forgiveness, wept, and embraced. They emerged walking hand-in-hand as they approached their waiting families. There was hugging, kissing, and laughing.

"The next night, the brothers sang a duet. Later, they traveled to a nearby city in the same car to share what God had done in their lives. They rejoiced and thanked God that He had delivered them from the bitterness of the past. Even the skeptical had to admit they had seen a miracle. The impact of these changed lives triggered an explosion of repentance, restitution, and love.

"Yet, the Derksen brothers could not have predicted what God was about to do. Even the most optimistic did not realize that this was the beginning of a revival that would affect thousands of people in Saskatoon and other cities in Canada. The movement popularly referred to as the 'Canadian Revival' was on."[1] ↑

---

1. Erwin W. Lutzer, *Flames of Freedom* (Chicago: Moody Press, 1976), 27–28. Used by permission.

downpour

self in the dirt:
a picture of repentance

self in the dirt:
a picture of repentance

PART 1

key verse to memorize

*"Godly grief produces a repentance that leads to salvation
without regret, whereas worldly grief produces death."*

2 Corinthians 7:10

For session 6 plans, turn to page 171 in the leader guide.

discussion guide on week 5: sin in the mirror, part 2

1. If God has been a "good and faithful friend" this week, share a brief testimony of how He has worked in your life.
2. Suppose someone asked you, "Does God really give people up to sin?" How would you respond? What Scriptures would you read?
3. What are some consequences of sin? How does God say He will respond to our rebellion?
4. What are the four steps down on the slippery slope of sin? What evidence in our society indicates that these describe human reality?
5. Volunteers: Without going into detail about the confidential things you confessed to others this week, describe your experience of the process and how has it been helpful or meaningful. Did it help get sin out in the open and secure prayer support for moving on to victory over the power of sin? How?

dvd session 6 message notes (29 minutes)

Scripture focus: 2 Corinthians 7:8-11

1. Repentance is a ___*Good*___ thing (2 Cor. 7:8-9).
   - It's not a bad thing to be _____ about sin. It's a good thing.
   Biblical Overview
   - John the Baptist (Matt. 3:2)
   - Disciples (Mark 6:12)
   - Joy in heaven over one sinner who repents (Luke 15:7)
   - Peter (Acts 2:38; 3:19)
   - Commanded (Acts 17:30)
   - God grants repentance (2 Tim. 2:25)
   - Jesus (Rev. 2:5,16; 3:19)
   - Example: the prodigal son (Luke 15:11-32)

downpour

snapshot summary

Repentance is a good thing, but it comes before revival. It is a recognition of sin for what it is, followed by heartfelt sorrow culminating in a change of behavior.

my goals for you

I want you to understand the value and necessity of repentance and show your godly sorrow over sin through acts of repentance.

Repentance is a change of heart in every way

Definition: Repentance is a _good thing (a recognition)_ of sin for what it is, followed by heartfelt sorrow culminating in a change of behavior.

See the sin chart on page 81.

Repentance before revival

Lindsay's testimony: a pattern of sin, hopelessness, and despair through repentance to freedom

responding to the message

1. Review by answering the following questions.
   a. How is repentance a good thing? How is grief over sin a good thing?
   b. What have you learned from New Testament Scriptures about the importance and necessity of repentance?
   c. Who are some leaders who preached messages of repentance?
   d. Who is the poster boy of repentance, and what did he do?
2. Review the definition of *repentance* above and discuss the three stages of repentance described in the definition. What are they?
3. Lindsay prayed, "Help me get out of this mess that I created for myself." Invite volunteers to share about a time they repented and won victory over sin. Focus not on the sin but on the process of confession and repentance: recognition, sorrow, and changed behavior.
4. Have volunteers pray sentence prayers that God will grant repentance.

preview statements for this week's study

- When we see afresh from God's Word where sin takes us, we should be ready to run in the other direction.
- Repentance is the funnel through which all personal revival flows.
- Repentance is the first step in a personal cleanup of the wreckage that sin brings.

Message-notes blanks: good, grieved, recognition, revival

| # Recognition of Sin, Part 1

1 **Fill in the blanks to define *repentance* as given in the DVD message (p. 79).**

Repentance is a recognition of _____ for what it is,

followed by heartfelt _____

culminating in a _____ of behavior.

When we see afresh from God's Word (like Rom. 1) where sin takes us, we should be ready to run in the other direction. Repentance begins with a recognition of sin for what it is. To help us do that, I want to review in more detail the kinds of sins that too often remain lodged in a believer's life. Here are three broad categories where you may need God to work.

Pride. Hardly anyone would disagree that pride is sin. Pride is the complete state of anti-God. It's self-centered thinking—I, me, my, mine, me first, all the time, nobody else. Acting-like-I'm-better-than-I-am, have-others-notice-me, don't-make-me-look-bad-or-I'll-make-you-pay pride.

Pleasure. Pleasure itself is not sin because God "richly supplies us with all things to enjoy" (1 Tim. 6:17, NASB). Pleasure becomes sin when we pursue it at the wrong time, with the wrong person, or in the wrong amount.

Priorities. This term describes the good left undone. Do you know to love your neighbor, pay your bills, walk with God, tell others about Jesus, and forgive when you are injured? Do you know to do these things? James 4:17 says, "Whoever knows the right thing to do and fails to do it, for him it is sin."

2 **Match the sin on the left with the correct definition on the right. Write a letter beside the number.**

_b_ 1. Pride   a. Leaving undone the good God has commanded

_c_ 2. Pleasure   b. Thinking too highly of myself and my interests

_a_ 3. Priorities   c. Pursuing something that feels good at the wrong time, with the wrong person, or in the wrong amount

(Answers: 1–b, 2–c, 3–a)

Pride, pleasure, and priorities are just three broad categories of sin. If we want to see sin in the mirror, we have to drill down into more detail. Can you handle it? This is the hard work many people are not doing, and the result is spiritual poverty we have come to call normal. So let's go after this with energy, believing that an outpouring of blessing and favor from God Himself is the reward on the other side of this look at personal sin. Under each of the three broad categories are three subcategories of sin in that area. Beyond that is a countless list of specifics. Let's preview. Then we'll dig.

PRIDE	PLEASURE	PRIORITIES
Position	Sex	Self
Prestige	Substance	Others
Power	Stuff	God

Pride

Position. "Finally I have the corner office." "I can't believe you asked me to do this. Don't you know who I am?" "Nobody talks to me like that." "I haven't worked as hard as I have to put up with ..." I think you get the picture. Position is thinking you're superior to others because of a role you have attained or a status you have achieved. It's the need to have your title mentioned or for everyone under you to salute as you pass. It can happen in the marketplace or even in your own home. It's the need to constantly remind others of who they are in relation to you.

Prestige. "More 'atta-boys' for me, please." "Tell me again how much you appreciate me and what I've done for you." "I want prizes and bonuses and thank-you notes and public acknowledgments." Prestige is a consuming need for recognition. It's the feeling that others are always watching and the insatiable thirst for others to pat you on the back. It's the insistence that nothing you do be overlooked or unrewarded by those in a position to do so. It's dropping names of prestigious associations; it's letting others know of your accomplishments; it's the constant concern that everyone know who you are.

Power. "When I say, 'Jump,' you ask, 'How high?'" "You are my daughter, and you'll do what I say." "I'm the boss, and don't you ever forget it." Power is the inappropriate use of influence. It's throttling up over someone else and using your words, your position, or your persona to force them to do something against their best interest. Worse, it's reveling in and glorying in the ability to affect others that way. Inappropriate displays of power and the love of power are incredibly destructive sins; God despises seeing these in His children.

❸ **Match the words and phrases on the left with the subcategories of pride they are associated with on the right. Write a letter beside the number.**

___ 1. Need for recognition	a. Position
___ 2. Refusal to do lowly jobs	b. Prestige
___ 3. Expectation of honor and respect	c. Power
___ 4. Expectation of obedience	
___ 5. Delight in being able to force others to follow	
___ 6. Name dropping to elevate your status by association	

(Answers: 1–b, 2–a, 3–a, 4–c, 5–c, 6–b)

You may have responded a little differently because these subcategories can overlap. Pride—thinking too highly of yourself and not highly enough of others—is the root sin at the bottom of many other sins.

4 Read the following Scripture and underline words that describe the demonstration of repentance from the sin of pride.

> *"Clothe yourselves, all of you, with humility toward one another, for God opposes the proud but gives grace to the humble. Humble yourselves, therefore, under the mighty hand of God so that at the proper time he may exalt you."*
> **1 Peter 5:5-6**

5 Beside each word or phrase below write a _P_ if it represents an action or attitude of pride or an _H_ if it represents an act of humbling yourself.

___ Demand your rights	___ Lay down your rights and wishes
___ Demand compliance	___ Cooperate
___ Assume subordinate role	___ Give God credit and glory
___ Serve others	___ Expect credit and recognition
___ Expect other to serve you	___ Manipulate to get your way
___ Condescending	___ Teachable
___ Accept lowly tasks	___ Confess your sins and needs
___ Offer praise to others	___ Insist on your way
___ Ask for prayer and help	___ Honor others above yourself

Ask the Lord to reveal any attitude or action in your life that exhibits pride and arrogance. Ask Him to forgive you. Ask Him to guide you and grant opportunities for you to humble yourself to uproot pride in your life. ✝

day 2 | Recognition of Sin, Part 2

1 Review the sin chart on page 81. List three subcategories of pride.

Pleasure

Sex. Not the good and the beautiful as God created but "my needs, what I want, when I want it. I don't care whom it hurts. I don't care whom it degrades. Everything for me." This sin, which is rampant and out of control in our world, is making serious headway in the church. A startling number of pastors and Christian leaders admit to private sexual addiction. Like a bad cavity, it eats away at the core of what following Christ really is. It's sin.

Substance abuse. Beware of any substance (legal or not) that dulls your need for God. Why do people drink so much alcohol? Why do people take drugs—legally or illegally? "They kind of dull the edge for me," you might say. "They soften the pain of life and keep me from experiencing the hard things in my life."

God doesn't want the edge of life softened. God wants you to experience it full-on. That's what shows you how much you need Him. God wants to fill up what's lacking in your capacity to cope with life. The great wickedness of substance abuse is that it keeps you from seeing how much you really need God. It doesn't matter if you have to have sugar or Starbucks or cigarettes; God does not want you to be under the power of anything other than Him (see 1 Cor. 6:12).

Stuff. It's not wrong to have things. It's wrong when things have you. Psalm 62:10 says, "If riches increase, set not your heart on them." When your life focuses on wanting things and living for stuff, then you've got a sin problem. Don't let stuff be the source of your greatest joy or satisfaction. Stuff pursued in the wrong amount or at the wrong time or for the wrong reasons is sin.

② **Give an example for each subcategory of sinful pleasure.**

Stuff: _____

Substance abuse: _____

Sex: _____

③ **As you read about priorities, underline words or phrases that identify issues to which you need to give special attention.**

Priorities

Priority of personal care. Sometimes sin is not taking care of yourself personally. Are you doing what you can to be healthy? Do you realize that your body is not your own but that you belong to God (see 1 Cor. 6:19-20)? Overeating, failure to exercise, and neglect of needed rest and relaxation are all sinful choices that reflect a wrong priority in the stewardship of your life for God. You may have heard the foolish statement "I'd rather burn out than rust out for God." As God's children we are required to care for this temple of the Holy Spirit, not in a preoccupied, consuming way but in a healthy, self-controlled way. To fail in time and health management is to leave the good undone, and that makes it sin. Do you need to confess it as such?

Priority of others. Do you make relationships a priority? How do you act when someone disappoints you or fails you? Are you becoming more loving? More forgiving? Kinder? More tenderhearted toward others (see Eph. 4:29-32)? This sin can be a failure to give ourselves to the people in our lives the way we should. Men, do we fail to open up and give ourselves to our wives in a way that is personally disclosing and emotionally satisfying to them? To close up and withhold yourself from your spouse, your children, or anyone in your life who needs you and can rightfully claim your time is sin.

Failure to forgive is often at the root of failing to love. "But you don't know what they did to me," you might say. I don't need to know. God knows. Forgiveness is a choice to release a person from the obligation that resulted when they injured you. Failing to forgive that person before God is sin. "Be kind to one another, tenderhearted, forgiving one another, as God in Christ forgave you" (Eph. 4:32). Failure to love, give myself to, and forgive those who injure me is failure to prioritize what matters to God—which is people. That failure is leaving that good priority undone, and it is sin.

Priority of your relationship with God. This is something only you and God can answer: Are you loving Christ with all your heart, soul, mind, and strength? If you go to a worship service and just watch others, you are withholding yourself from God—it's sin.

Are you walking with God? You know that it's good to spend time in prayer and Bible study every day, but are you doing that? If you know it's good and you don't do it, it's sin.

Sin can be dealt with only when we call it what it really is. Stop for a moment and say these words out loud: "It's sin." Say it again: "It's sin." Cultivate the discipline of calling your behavior that fails to keep God's law what it really is—it's sin.

> Only you can answer what categories of sin are convicting you. Read the list again and ask God to show you where you need to focus in adjusting your priorities. He will. He sincerely wants you to be free from sin and to move under the refreshing downpour of His favor. ✝

day 3 | Heartfelt Sorrow

1 We've been working with a definition of *repentance.* Do you remember the three parts? We just covered the first one. See if you can fill in the blanks below. If you need help, take a peek at the definition on page 79.

(1) Repentance is a recognition of _____ for what it is,

(2) followed by heartfelt _____

(3) culminating in a _____ of behavior.

I have to say I've been excited to get to this stage in the process with you. This is the time when we move from learning *about* downpour to *experiencing* it firsthand. If you respond to the Lord in repentance, you will be under a downpour of mercy and forgiveness. You will find yourself joyfully laughing in the rain in the very near future.

The absolutely essential thought in all this is repentance. Repentance is the funnel through which all personal revival flows. Repentance is the natural next step on our journey. We have seen God's holiness exalted before our eyes. We have been brought to a place of personal brokenness about our sin and the tsunami of consequences that devastate our experience as the after-shock of personal sin. Repentance is the first step in a personal cleanup of the wreckage that sin brings. Refusing repentance only takes us down and never takes us up. Denial of sin only takes us backward and never forward. Repentance alone opens the way to a fresh outpouring of God's favor in our lives. No wonder repentance is such a common theme in God's Word.

Repentance Is a Good Thing

Trust me on this one: you want more repentance in your life. Though it's not an easy or pleasant thing, it's a *good* thing. If you want to get to a better place with God, get repentance.

The church in Corinth was the most problematic church in the New Testament era. In 2 Corinthians Paul pleaded with them to halt their sinful behavior. In 2 Corinthians 7:8 Paul refers to an earlier corrective letter he had written them: "Even if I made you grieve with my letter, I do not regret it." Apparently, the earlier letter was to the point, as in, "Hey, repent or else! I mean it; knock it off and repent, or you're going to get it big time!"

Paul may have had moments of doubt about his strong rebuke, because he said he regretted it. Maybe he wondered, *Did I say too much? Was I too hard on them?* But deep down he knew that leading them to a place of grief over their sin was for their own benefit. It's good for us to feel sorrow over our wrong choices. It's right to feel grief over sin because that can lead us to very important choices. We don't get to a better place with God until we recognize that where we are is not good.

Sometimes we have to receive a hard word, something we'd rather not hear, in order to get to the place we've always wanted to be. Paul felt that tension after he had written this strong letter of rebuke. Then he said, "I do not regret it—though I did regret it, for I see that that letter grieved you." Apparently, they were wounded by the truth, but it was only temporary. Eventually, they repented, and that was the cause of Paul's rejoicing (see v. 9).

❷ Why is repentance a good thing? Check a response or write your own.
- ❏ a. Repentance is the trip back to joy and vitality in my walk with the Lord.
- ❏ b. Repentance is getting away from the slime and filth of a sinful life.
- ❏ c. Repentance is leaving the hurtful place where I suffer from the consequences of my sin.
- ❏ d. Repentance is the way I move into a life that pleases and brings glory to my Heavenly Father.
- ❏ e. Other: _____

You could have checked any one of those reasons. They are all reasons repentance is a good thing.

Week after week I stand at the front of our worship center after the service and pray with people, many of whom are grieving over their sin. In my heart I feel compassion for their pain, but I don't want to short-circuit what God is doing in their hearts. In my flesh I want to say, "It's OK; don't be so upset about what you've done." But I know they need to feel grief over sin in order to fully experience God's grace. Paul rejoiced because he knew that only when the Corinthian Christians were wounded by the reality of their sinful choices could they begin to experience the renewing power of His Spirit at work in their lives. Paul rejoiced, "not because you were grieved, but because you were grieved into repenting" (2 Cor. 7:9).

The truth of these messages, "Sin in the Mirror" and "Self in the Dirt," can lead each of us to a changed life through repentance. This life change makes hearing the hard truth not only worthwhile but also a cause for rejoicing. No doubt about it, repentance is a very good thing.

Repentance is the moment when everything changes. God is not reluctant or unwilling to unleash a downpour of blessing on your life. Even now the clouds of heaven are bursting with His grace and mercy of God, which will shower on your parched heart at the moment of genuine repentance. Picture it now by faith: all of God's favor, all of God's grace, all of God's blessing, curling like a mighty wave and breaking on the shore of your life. This comes only through repentance.

Look back over the sin list on page 67 and the chart on page 81. Invite God to develop in your spirit a deep grief over your sin. Not a sorry-I-got-caught attitude but a sorry-I've-offended-and-brought-discredit-to-the-one-I-love kind of grief. Ask for the kind of grief He knows leads to repentance that leaves no regrets. Remember that Jesus had to go to the cross and suffer and die because of your sin. Pursue the Lord for this gift of godly sorrow that leads to genuine repentance. Grieve over sin. ↑

day 4 | A Change in Behavior

❶ Review again our definition of *repentance.* See if you can fill in the blanks below. I've added a few, so take a peek at the definition on page 79 if you need help.

(1) Repentance is a _____ of _____ for what it is,

(2) followed by _____ _____

(3) culminating in a _____ of _____.

Jesus and Repentance

In Revelation 2:5 Jesus says, "Remember therefore from where you have fallen; repent." Do you ever think, *I thought by now I'd be further along in my spiritual life; what should I do?* Do this: repent. Wake up to the reality that you're not progressing as you want in your faith because some things in your life need to change—and that happens through repentance. You may think, *My life was a mess until I found the Lord, and I was so close to Him for a while; but then I started to wander. What does He want me to do now?* Repent and return to the way you saw yourself, your sin, and God's holy requirements when you first turned to Him.

This is the heart of Christ for the church today, even if it takes drastic measures. In Revelation 2:16 the Lord says to the church, "Repent. If not, I will come to you soon and war against them with the sword of my mouth." Jesus Christ Himself is moving today in resistance against every person who does not humble himself and repent of his sins. "That doesn't sound like the Jesus I hear preached about so often today," you may be saying. Too often Jesus is characterized as an overindulgent parent: "Of course you can have whatever you want. Of course I'll answer your prayers as soon as you think I should. Here, have another cupcake." Those are words we put in the Savior's mouth, but now hear what He really says: "As many as I love, I *rebuke and chasten*. Therefore be zealous and repent" (Rev. 3:19, NKJV, emphasis added).

2 **Which statement reflects Jesus's desire for you? Check one.**
   ❏ a. "Enjoy yourself and have another cupcake."
   ❏ b. "Repent of your sinful ways and turn back to your first love for Me."

I don't know what your life has been like. I don't know where you've been or what you've done. You may have chosen some paths you're not proud of or done some things you would be ashamed for others to know. Believe me on this: God can and will wipe away all that shame and sadness if you will only repent: "Come now, let us reason together, says the LORD: though your sins are like scarlet, they shall be as white as snow; though they are red like crimson, they shall become like wool" (Isa. 1:18). How can that happen? How can you leave your past behind you? The answer is the bull's-eye we're shooting for: repentance.

Repentance Is Change Inside Me That Shows in My Actions
Repentance is change in every way and at every level. Repentance is change in me—not a change of spouse, not a change of job, not a change of where I live or whom I hang out with. Repentance is change in the place where it's needed most—inside me. If you study all of the Hebrew and Greek terms together, you get this three-part definition:

Repentance is a recognition of sin for what it is, followed by heartfelt sorrow culminating in a change of behavior.

I see sin for what it is—changing my mind. I experience heartfelt sorrow—changing my heart (or emotions). I determine to change my behavior—changing my will. Repentance is change at every level of your being—in your mind, your heart, and your will.

③ Match the step of repentance on the left with the correct change required on the right. Write a letter beside the number.

___ 1. Recognition of sin   a. Change in my will

___ 2. Heartfelt sorrow   b. Change in my mind

___ 3. Change in behavior   c. Change in my heart

(Answers: 1–b, 2–c, 3–a)

The prodigal son is the poster boy of repentance. It's all in Luke 15. This know-it-all kid came up with a rebellious plan. He demanded of his father all the money from his inheritance in order to live the life of his dreams. Apparently, the father was permissive, because he did what the son asked. Then according to Luke 15:13, the son "squandered his property in reckless living." He was a party animal, and he ended up living with the animals. One day he was so hungry that he craved the pigs' food. The life of his dreams? More like a nightmare on the pig farm!

Then he woke up (step 1). Luke 15:17 says, "He came to himself" or came to his senses. He recognized the sin in his life for what it was—that is the first step to repentance: changing your mind about sin. Next he said to his father, "I am no longer worthy to be called your son" (v. 19). Feeling shame over his actions and more like a slave than a son, he changed his heart about sin (step 2). Then the prodigal son said, "I will arise and go to my father, and I will say to him …" (v. 18). That was a change of his will, resulting in a change of behavior (step 3).

That son who a short time before thought sin was so attractive; who felt a right to whatever satisfaction he craved, no matter whom it hurt; and who couldn't wait to get as far as possible from his family—that son repented, and everything changed. His thoughts changed; his feelings changed; his actions changed.

④ Complete the sentences below by filling in the blanks with the kind of change required in each step of repentance. Choose from the words *will*, *mind*, and *heart*.

1. Recognition of sin requires a change in my _____ .

2. Heartfelt sorrow requires a change in my _____ .

3. Change in behavior is a change in my _____ .

Repentance involves a change in your mind (recognition of sin), in your heart or emotions (heartfelt sorrow), and in your will (producing a specific plan of action for change).

❧ **Spend private, intimate time with the Lord on this subject of your specific sins. I told you that this repentance thing would not be easy, but there's no going forward unless we do it right. And don't put off this step, or you'll soon be lost in that barren wasteland again—dry and distant from God. Go to the Lord in prayer and do your part now. ✝**

| # Jonah's Personal Revival

1 **Read Jonah 1–3. As you read chapter 3, pay attention to the manner in which the city repented. Then read the picture of personal revival from the life of Jonah on page 90.**

2 **When did Jonah choose to repent and obey God's commission?**
- ❏ a. When he began to feel guilty for running away from the assignment
- ❏ b. When the storm became life-threatening
- ❏ c. As soon as the sailors threw him into the sea
- ❏ d. After three days in the belly of the great fish

Recognizing your sin is not repentance. Feeling sorrow for getting caught or because of the severe consequences of your sin is not repentance. Even confessing your sin by agreeing with God that you've been wrong is not repentance. Jonah demonstrated repentance when he obeyed the second time God gave him the assignment.

When Jonah repented, God had an instrument He could work through. Imagine having a revival crusade at which 120,000 people get saved.

3 **What did the people of Nineveh do to repent? Check all that apply.**
- ❏ a. They held a feast and celebrated in worship.
- ❏ b. They fasted and prayed for God's forgiveness and mercy.
- ❏ c. They killed Jonah for preaching a harsh message against the people.
- ❏ d. They put on sackcloth and ashes.
- ❏ e. They turned from their violence and evil ways.

4 **After which of these actions did God relent from the disaster He had planned for the city? Circle the letter above.**

The people of Nineveh, from the king and nobles to the most common people, fasted, put on sackcloth and ashes, cried out for mercy, and turned from their evil ways. God noticed the humility in their fasting and wearing sackcloth. He heard their cries for mercy. But God relented when they turned from their evil ways (e). Are you encouraged to know that even a pagan city can understand God's requirements for repentance and get it right?

Read 2 Timothy 2:25-26 below and pray that God will grant you genuine repentance. Don't wait for disasters or storms before you return.

"God may perhaps grant them repentance leading to a knowledge of the truth, and they may escape from the snare of the devil, after being captured by him to do his will" (2 Tim. 2:25-26). ✦

From the Life of Jonah: A Picture of Repentance

JONAH 1–3; ROMANS 2:2–4

Who doesn't love hearing testimonies about what God has done in people's lives? Just set up the microphones and get comfortable; we could listen all day. That is, unless these people boasting of God's grace have hurt us, or worse, have hurt the ones we love. What do we do when justice seems unseated and silent? Instead of listening and rejoicing over God's grace, we bring down the judge's gavel. Grace is too good for them.

Such was the mind-set of Jonah that sent him on his infamous Mediterranean cruise. More than just disobedient, Jonah thought in some silly, small way that he could keep God's kindness from reaching his enemies. Jonah had pronounced himself their judge, and no one could object—Nineveh didn't deserve God's mercy. But somewhere in the bowels of the fish, Jonah realized that he didn't either.

There in that protected, surreal, secret place, God finally got Jonah's attention. He could have let Jonah drown. He could have let him endure a second-rate life in Tarshish. But in His kindness God went after full reversal. He put Jonah in a place where he would finally grieve over his sin and recognize that he was to blame for his own wrong choices.

Now Jonah didn't think he was ever coming out of that fish. Read his prayer in Jonah 2, and you hear a man wrapping up the last moments of his life. Jonah thought, *I'm going to be standing before God in just a moment, so I'd better get right with Him now.* Jonah had no idea what God had prepared to do the moment he repented.

So it didn't take long for the spit-up, bleached-out, poster boy of the second chance to get on the road to Nineveh once his heart had returned to God. As he had promised, Jonah proclaimed God's great salvation to the people he loathed, and he watched God rain a downpour of mercy on the wicked. Jonah's call to "repent or else" coursed like a mighty river through the streets of the vast city. And as Jonah preached doom, the people understood the righteous anger of a holy God, turned from their wicked ways, and repented in sackcloth and ashes. From the greatest to the least, the people of Nineveh threw themselves on God's mercy. And God heard their cry.

With the same outrageous grace that spared Jonah, God now spared Nineveh. His kindness drew the people to repentance, and His mercy overruled revenge. As hearts were revived, they recognized their sin for what it was and humbled themselves under God's mighty hand. And to no one's surprise, God stepped toward them with open arms. ↑

self in the dirt:
a picture of repentance

PART 2

self in the dirt:
a picture of repentance

PART 2

key verse to memorize

*"Repent therefore, and turn again, that your sins
may be blotted out, that times of refreshing may
come from the presence of the Lord."*

Acts 3:19-20

For session 7 plans, turn to page 172 in the leader guide.

discussion guide on week 6: self in the dirt, part 1

1. What are the three parts of our definition of *repentance?*
2. See if your group can name the three categories of sin and the three subcategories under each. (Write them on a marker board or chart paper.)
3. Define *pride* and give examples for each subcategory of pride (p. 81).
4. Review your answers to activity 5 on page 82. What are some ways you can humble yourself to dig out the root sin of pride?
5. Define the sins related to pleasure and priorities and give examples for each of the subcategories (see day 2).
6. How can repentance be a good thing? Share your responses to activity 2 on page 85.
7. What do you do in repentance to demonstrate (1) a change of your mind, (2) a change of your heart or emotions, and (3) a change of your will?

dvd session 7 message notes (27 minutes)

Scripture focus: 2 Corinthians 7:9-11

I'll know I've repented when—

    a. there are deeds appropriate to repentance (Acts 26:20);

    b. I bear fruits of repentance (Luke 3:8).

Five Marks of Genuine Repentance (2 Cor. 7:9-11)

1. _Grief_ over sin (2 Cor. 7:9-11)

    a. Feelings accompany repentance. *Sorrow*

    b. True contact with God produces a feeling of unworthiness.

        Abraham (Gen. 18:27); Job (Job 42:6); Isaiah (Isa. 6:5);

            Peter (Luke 5:8); John (Rev. 1:17)

    c. Let's get specific about sin (see the chart on p. 81).

2. _Strong Repulsion_ toward sin (2 Cor. 7:11)

downpour

*Position
Prestige
Power*

snapshot summary

Five marks of genuine repentance include grief over sin, repulsion toward sin, restitution toward others, revival toward God, and moving forward.

my goals for you

I want you to understand the nature of genuine repentance and to show your eagerness for a right relationship with God by repenting.

3. ___restitution___ toward others (2 Cor. 7:11)
   a. Fixing the fallout of sin; Zacchaeus (Luke 19:1-10)
   b. You can't be right with God if you don't want to be right with the people your sin has injured.
   c. You don't go and ask forgiveness from someone who sinned against you.
4. ___revival___ toward God (2 Cor. 7:11)
5. Moving ___forward___ (2 Cor. 7:9-10)
   a. Not looking back
   b. Breaking the chains of the failures of the past

🔘 Message music: see the "Beautiful God" lyrics on page 94.

responding to the message

1. Review by answering the following questions.
   a. What are deeds (Acts 26:20) and fruits (Luke 3:8) of repentance? Take turns naming a sin and having someone else describe a fruit of repentance for that sin. (For example: theft—returning what was stolen, asking forgiveness, and accepting the consequences)
   b. What are the five marks of repentance? Give an example of each one.
2. Return to your small groups of three persons (of the same gender). Give updates about the ways God is granting victory over sin. Once again ask, *How may we pray for you?* and pray for each person in the group.

preview statements for this week's study

- If you are repentant, others will be able to see it in your life.
- True repentance is heartfelt sadness about what you've done to God.
- Revival brings more of God in your life, experienced and enjoyed.

Message-notes blanks: Grief, Repulsion, Restitution, Revival, Forward

Beautiful God

closer to Your throne, I'm crawling / <u>i blew it</u> on my own, but You're calling
welcoming me home, and I wonder / what could You be thinking?

beautiful God, did not I surprise You
or catch You off guard when I disobeyed You?
I know I deserve a life without You
but there You are with open arms, beautiful God

deep inside my heart You see / each deceptive part, but You love me
and I cannot believe Your mercy / and how do You do that?

oh, Your grace overwhelms me / like a river floods the plains
oh, Your mercy washes over me / i sing, "Holy is Your name"

"While we were still weak, at the right time Christ died for the ungodly. ... God shows his love for us in that while we were still sinners, Christ died for us. Since, therefore, we have now been justified by his blood, much more shall we be saved by him from the wrath of God. ... We also rejoice in God through our Lord Jesus Christ, through whom we have now received reconciliation."
Romans 5:6-11

Slowly read the song lyrics above and meditate on their meaning.
Use the following questions to deepen your love for the beautiful
God who loves and forgives you.
1. What are some reasons you do not deserve His love and forgiveness?
   Underline words or phrases. I've underlined one for you.
2. In what unbelievable ways God has responded to you? Circle those
   words or phrases, like *welcoming me home.*

This week listen to the song on your Message-Music CD (track 4) at the
back of this book and worship God for His great love, mercy, and beauty.

Pray prayers of thanksgiving and express to the Lord your love for Him
in response to His great love and sacrifice for you.

| # Repentance

At the end of this week you will find specific exercises to help you in the crisis of repentance. These activities are sparks to start the fire of your repentant conversation with God. What you won't find are "Five Easy Steps to Repentance" or "30 Days to a More Repentant You." Only God can give you a repentant heart. In fact, 2 Timothy 2:25 says, "God may perhaps *grant* them repentance" (emphasis added). Repentance is a gift God gives to a person who wholeheartedly seeks Him. Maybe as you've been reading, you've said to yourself, *But I don't feel grief over my sin.* God will help you with that if you ask Him. Maybe you even believe your actions or attitudes are not wrong, even though God's Word says they are. Again, you desperately to seek God and ask Him to change your mind about that.

> **Pause and ask the Lord to grant the repentance you need. Give Him permission to convict of sin, give you godly sorrow for your sin, and guide you to turn from your sin to a life that pleases Him.**

All in all, repentance is not easy. If it were, everyone would do it. Instead, we have a worldly church struggling to build the kingdom in its own strength and failing miserably at its primary job—to display the power and glory of Jesus Christ. Too many impressive churches don't impress lost people with the impressiveness of all Jesus is and longs to be for them.

Only God can grant us repentance about all we have done and failed to do. I don't have any quick fixes to give you here. However, I can tell you how to know for sure that genuine repentance has taken place in your life.

Five Marks of Genuine Repentance

If we could hang out together for an extended time, I would know whether you are repentant, and you would know the same of me. Specific marks characterize the behavior of a person who truly repents. I write this not on my own authority but on the authority of God's Word.

These marks are called fruits of repentance. Acts 26:20 qualifies them as deeds appropriate to repentance: "Repent and turn to God, performing deeds in keeping with their repentance." Luke 3:8 says, "Bear fruits in keeping with repentance." If you are repentant, others will be able to see it in your life. Your actions will show your heart. Repentance is the unseen, underground root that will eventually produce fruit in your life that will be apparent to everyone—including you. What are these fruits of repentance?

In 2 Corinthians 7:9-11 Paul lists 11 fruits in random order. But for our study I've grouped them here under five headings in the order I believe a repentant person experiences them:

1. Grief over sin (vv. 9-11)
2. Repulsion toward sin (v. 11)
3. Restitution toward others (v. 11)
4. Revival toward God (v. 11)
5. Moving forward (vv. 9-10)

Mark 1: Grief over Sin

This one is hard to miss in our text. Paul says in 2 Corinthians 7:9, "You felt a godly grief," then again in verse 10, "Godly grief produces a repentance that leads to salvation." The word *grief* is the Greek word *lupeo*. It's the "greatly distressed" feeling the disciples had when Jesus announced His crucifixion in Matthew 17:23. This word for *grief* or *sorrow* is used 26 times in the New Testament. Half of those occurrences are in 2 Corinthians, with half of them in this passage. That fact makes this passage the most concentrated statement in all of Scripture about the feelings that accompany repentance.

If you're really repentant, you will feel some things. You'll feel grief over sin; you will feel internal hurting or soul anguish. When you're convicted of sin, you will feel grief and shame about the wrong choice you made.

True repentance is heartfelt sadness about what I've done to God. At the heart of every choice to sin is a rejection of God, and that's why the grief of repentance must begin with the way my actions affect the Lord. When I choose the wrong, I'm really saying, "You're not enough, God. I need this too. You have not met my needs, so I'm going out on my own this time." Repentance is happening in your heart when you begin to express through your grief, "How can I spit in the face of mercy? How can I slap away the hand of God's grace? God reaches out to bless me, and I shun His merciful love."

Repentance is detecting the lie that aided my sinful choice and destroying it. Repentance is grief over that lie I told myself and the choice I made because of it. Repentance shows up in my wounded spirit. How could I have acted that way toward God? How could I treat His love so poorly when He's given me so much? Real repentance recognizes that my sin is against God.

But watch out. Worldly grief can become a poor substitute for the real thing. Worldly grief is "Sorry I got caught. Sorry I feel so bad. Sorry I look so bad. Sorry You don't like this, God. God, You're not right; You're not good; You're not enough for me."

1 **Identify the difference between worldly grief (the substitute) and godly grief that leads to genuine repentance. Write the word *godly* or *worldly* beside each of these responses to sin.**

____W____ a. I'm sorry I feel so bad.
____G____ b. How could I have done that?
____G____ c. I feel sickened by my choice.
____W____ d. I'm sorry I got caught.
____W____ e. I feel sickened by the consequence.
____W____ f. I'm sorry I don't look good in this.
____W____ g. I'm sorry You don't like this, God.
____G____ h. I'm sad about what I've done to God.
____G____ i. How could I have acted like that?
____G____ j. I feel wounded in my spirit.

(Answers: godly–b, c, h, i, j; worldly–a, d, e, f, g)

2 **Review our chart of sins. Consider the categories of pride, pleasure, and priorities. Do you feel grief over anything in those categories? Will you allow God's Spirit to bring you to a place of heartfelt grief about specific patterns in your life?**

downpour

PRIDE	PLEASURE	PRIORITIES
Position	Sex	Self
Prestige	Substance	Others
Power	Stuff	God

If you can't, then you're not repenting. Without repentance you will never experience a downpour of God's awesome presence—not under any circumstances. It just won't come without repentance.

> Whatever holds you back from this downpour, bring it to God now and sincerely ask for the heartfelt grief He requires. Sincerely ask, "Lord, show me my sin," "Reveal to me how You see my sin," or "Bring me to the place where I experience Your sorrow over my sin." ↑

day 2 | Repulsion and Restitution

1 What is the first mark of genuine repentance you studied yesterday?

_____

Mark 2: Repulsion Toward Sin

Grief over sin leads very quickly to feelings of repulsion about that sin. Notice that Paul says in 2 Corinthians 7:11, "See what earnestness this godly grief has produced in you." The word *earnestness* implies diligence. When I'm really repentant, I have serious energy about putting sin behind me. Repentance brings with it a new urgency about my relationship with God and strong negative feelings toward anything that would injure it. What used to be so attractive to me now repulses me. I'm indignant about it. I'm strongly opposed to it and resolutely determined that it will always be repulsive in my eyes.

2 Below are some synonyms for *repulsive*. Circle four words that help you best understand how you need to feel about your sin.

- abhorrent
- appalling
- disgusting
- creepy
- foul
- gross
- hideous
- horrid
- loathsome
- nasty
- nauseating
- obnoxious
- revolting
- sickening
- vile

Repentance is feeling that way about our sin. You look at what you used to do and say, "Yuck!" It makes you gag to think of what you once thought could bring you joy. "I don't want to act like that anymore," you say. "I don't want to say those things. When will I grow up and put that behind me once and for all?" Repentance is when whatever private satisfaction a specific sin brought me now makes me want to vomit because I see it for what it really is.

❸ Grief over sin is one mark of genuine repentance. What is the second?

_____

Mark 3: Restitution Toward Others

When repentance occurs in your heart, you will have an immediate, urgent desire to contact the people your sin has wounded and fix the fallout. Repentance is when you don't just want to be right with God; you want to be reconciled with the people your sin has injured. It's a fruit of repentance. Some Bible translations call this "avenging of wrong" (2 Cor. 7:11, NASB) and "readiness to see justice done" (2 Cor. 7:11, NIV).

Zacchaeus is famous for making restitution. As a tax collector he was in a position to steal whatever he could from everyone he worked with. When he repented, the first action he took was to make things right with those his sin had injured. "Man, this money doesn't belong to me," he said. "I've got to give it back. I don't want this at my house" (Luke 19:1-10, author's paraphrase).

Restitution is a mark of genuine repentance. That's why Paul commended the eagerness of the Corinthians to clear themselves. That word *eagerness* in Greek is *apologia*. It's the idea from which we get *apologetics,* which means *to give an explanation or reason.* Restitution involves going to a person and saying, "What I did [or said] to you was wrong. I'm truly sorry I did that. I don't have any excuses. Will you forgive me?" Restitution makes every effort possible to restore what was taken or ruined by sin.

❹ Read each of the following responses made attempting to reconcile with a person injured by sin. Write *R* beside the statements that express appropriate restitution. Leave blank the ones that fall short.

_R_ 1. You falsely claimed personal expenses on a company travel-expense report. You confess to your boss and give him a check to reimburse the personal expenses.

___ 2. You borrowed some yard tools from a neighbor and later moved out of town without returning them. Because it will be very expensive to return them, you decide only to send him a note saying you are sorry.

_R_ 3. You lied to your parents, and your sister was punished. You tell the truth to your parents, ask your sister for forgiveness, and deliver a special gift to try and compensate for her unjust punishment.

_R_ 4. After declaring bankruptcy years ago, you begin to prosper. Though the law does not require it, you repay your original creditors.

___ 5. You said hurtful, untrue things about your spouse in front of your children. To protect your image, you ask your spouse's forgiveness only privately, so your children never know the truth.

(Answers: R–1, 3, 4)

Restitution seeks to do as much as possible to undo the harm caused by the sin even when it is costly to do so. Repentance is immediately concerned about the people your sin has injured. That's why Paul says in verse 11, "What earnestness ... what eagerness to clear yourselves. ... At every point you have proved yourself innocent in the matter." *Innocent* means *free of guilt, blameless in the eyes of others.* You deal with your sin with the people your sin injured. Your spouse, your children, your boss, your neighbor, your faithful friend—all of these people now gladly report that you have done what you can to restore the fallout your sin caused between you and them.

As you look in the rearview mirror of your life, maybe you've said or done things that if others knew, you would feel incredibly ashamed. Maybe you carry those memories like a 10-ton weight on your back. Good news: that weight can be lifted! Through repentance you can experience God's incredible grace and all-consuming forgiveness. You can break the chains to your past and go forward into a glorious future—but it involves restitution. Whether your sin is large or small, you can be cleansed, you can be forgiven, you can be on a new, clean page under God's grace. But you have to go all the way in repentance—which means making restitution.

Restitution, when seriously contemplated, can raise fear in our hearts. What if they don't say anything? What if they tell me to get off their front porch? Yes, you run the risk of their rejection, but then you will have done everything you know to do, and you can leave their reaction with God. Do the best you can to build the bridge of reconciliation. No more excuses. No more blame shifting. Take responsibility for restitution. Go straight to that person and do all you can to make it right.

But what if I go to jail or get fired? You have a choice: carry the load of guilt for the rest of your life or make things right and accept (or pay) the consequences of your sin. Forgiveness, freedom from guilt, and a clear conscience can be priceless!

⑤ List the first three marks of genuine repentance.

Mark 1: *Grief*

Mark 2: *Repulsion*

Mark 3: *Restitution change behavior*

Mark 4: Revival toward God

Mark 5: Moving forward

Repentance—mind, emotions, and will. No more rationalizing, no more excusing, no more blaming others. If that's really happening in your life, there will be grief over sin, there will be repulsion toward sin, and there will be restitution toward others.

🙏 **Pray that God will reveal to you every sin that requires restitution. Ask Him to make clear the steps you need to take to make things right. Pray for the courage and strength to pay the price of restitution, no matter the cost.** ✝

Revival and Moving Forward

Mark 4: Revival Toward God

Like a river rushing down a mountainside, like a waterfall from a cool stream, God's mercy will now begin to wash over your life. Repentance will bring an obvious restoration of your relationship with the Lord. Your heart will become very sensitive to sin, and you will experience an increased capacity to rejoice in God's blessings. You'll hunger more for God's Word and crave things of the flesh less. Paul points this out as he continues his description of genuine repentance.

Paul characterizes the Corinthians' renewed relationship with God in the words "What fear" (2 Cor. 7:11). Previously, the Corinthians were involved in all kinds of sexual sin, and they didn't care what God thought. Their genuine repentance had increased in them "the fear of the Lord."

Fear is the attitude of heart that seeks a right relationship with the source of the fear. If I'm afraid of fire, I stand back a bit. If I'm afraid of water, I don't go in over my head. If I fear God, I'm very careful to do exactly as He asks, as quickly as I can. Fear of God is a good thing. "The fear of the LORD is the beginning of wisdom," says Proverbs 9:10. Every revived heart has an increased sense of God's nearness and our accountability to Him. The biblical term for that increased awe or respect is *fear,* and Paul observed that in the repentant Corinthians.

Paul also observed the revival flowing from their repentant hearts as an increased passion for the things of the Lord. He marveled, "What longing, what zeal" (2 Cor. 7:11). All of a sudden, church isn't a chore anymore for the repentant person. Bible study is not a burden. You delight in all God and His people and His Word have for you.

Zeal in the revived heart is an increased passion for the things of God. Life is not drudgery anymore. It doesn't matter what's in the newspaper this week or what's coming around the next corner. The revived person finds joy in every situation because he remembers this thing called life is only temporary. We're going to heaven someday! And until then, each breath is for God. This joy is a big part of revival. Remember our definition? Revival is renewed interest after a period of indifference or decline. Revival brings more of God in your life, experienced and enjoyed.

❶ **What is the fourth mark of genuine repentance?**

Revival toward God

Mark 5: Moving Forward

Here's the final mark of genuine repentance: moving forward and not looking back. Many people spend their lives lamenting what they see in the rearview mirror. If you're thinking, *Oh, if I had chosen differently when I was in college, if only I had not … if I had just quit … if I hadn't gone there. Why did I do that? Why am I like this?* Many people have their lives sadly submerged in a sea of regret—what might have been. It's easy to spot people who haven't

downpour

repented: they live in the past. They're stuck. Everyday is about reviewing a series of tragic circumstances that lock their focus on what is already done. I hope this doesn't describe you.

Genuine repentance also eliminates that persistent regret: "Godly grief produces a repentance ... without regret" (v. 10). When repentance is genuine, the human heart experiences cleansing, and by God's grace it moves beyond the kind of self-punishment that's stuck in the past and can't or won't move into the future. You know repentance is truly happening in your heart when you get locked in on what's ahead and experience freedom from what's behind.

That's why Paul says in verse 9, "... so that you suffered no loss through us." Repentance never takes you to a bad place. Repentance is never a waste of time; it is never a shortfall or a write-off; it's not a ceaseless cycle of worldly regret. Paul reminded the Corinthians that repentance was not a loss to them but actually a gain because it got them out of the rut of a self-condemning past and moved them forward into the freshness of a revived relationship with God. "Today is the first day of the rest of my life." When you can say that and mean it from your heart, it's a fruit of repentance.

② Grief, repulsion, restitution, and revival are four marks of genuine repentance. What is the fifth mark of genuine repentance?

Moving Forward

OK, that's it. I can't say any more about holiness, sin, and repentance. The ball is in your court now. All the information is on the table and available for your active embrace. Take time now to actually express repentance about the sin God has shown you in the mirror of your own life. If you do that now with all your energy, the raindrops of restoration and revival will begin to fall on you. By faith I see the clouds of mercy forming. Now go for it!

Activate

Do you want revival? Radical change calls for a radical response. Now that we've explored five marks of genuine repentance, let's make them personal.

Review your list of personal sins God showed you "in the mirror" (p. 67) and the categories of sin on page 81. Go to God with this list. Tell Him (or copy this into your journal):

Lord, I'm so sorry for this sin of _pride_ [be very specific]. I confess this to You as sin; I say it out loud: _pride_ is sin. I have been excusing _pride_ in my life with the reasoning that _____ made it justifiable. I used to think I was pretty good, that I just needed some minor adjustments. Now I see _____. I now reverse those rationalizations by honestly confessing that You have been right all along. _pride_ is sin, and I have no excuse. I bring it into the light of Your truth. I'm so sorry, Lord, and I humbly ask Your forgiveness. Help me as I turn from this sin. ✝

| # The Hardest Work

Replicate

The best way to impact the lives of others is to make things right with those your sin has injured. That work is called restitution. Let me be totally transparent and tell you it will be the hardest part of this book for most who read it. But it will also produce the most genuine and lasting parts of personal revival.

1 **In your journal or in a separate notebook make a restitution chart or use a separate page for each person. Include for the following information.**
   1. Name
   2. Offense(s) (your offenses, not theirs)
   3. Action needed/restitution required
   4. When can I do this?

Ask yourself, *To whom do I need to write a letter of apology? Whom do I need to call and ask forgiveness? Whom do I need to visit?* Complete the chart, being very specific. In the context of the entire problem, your wrong may not even be the biggest piece, but it is your piece to make right. You are repenting first before God (vertical) and then before the person whom your sin hurt (horizontal). This is unconditional repentance, not at all dependent on their response.

Restitution may mean more than an apology. Consider what your sin has cost them—money, reputation, and so on. Pay it back as far as you are able. Also write down when you are going to contact the person and how you are going to do so.

2 **Ask a friend or mentor to give you prayer support as you follow through with this step. Report to them the results of your restitution efforts. Trust me when I tell you that this will be one of the greatest blessings you have ever experienced.**

⟩ Elevate
After you have begun doing the hard work of repenting and making restitution, give thanks:

Lord, thank You for changing my heart. You have produced a deep grief in me over what I've done. I have excused the inexcusable and blamed others for what I'm responsible for. I see that as sin now, and I'm turning around. As best as I know how, I'm repenting of all the things that have kept me dry and distant from You. It makes me sick just to think of how I've grieved You.

By Your grace I am dealing with it now. Already I sense that You are welling up in me the hope of restoration and the rightness of reconciliation to You. Don't stop, Lord! I am performing deeds in keeping with repentance. Thank You for this renewed season of mercy to get this work done. I'm getting on the right road, and I'm not looking back. This I pray in Jesus' name. Amen. ✝

downpour

| # Personal Revival in Wales

1 Read on page 104 about the picture of personal revival sparked by Evan Roberts in Wales. Pay attention to the fruits of revival that became evident in the communities touched by revival.

2 List evidences in the communities that God was granting repentance in the lives of the people.

_____

_____

3 What prayer of Evan's indicated his desire to humble himself and rid himself of pride and hidden sin?

_____

4 Review the four points in Evan's message and see if you need to obey these points for personal revival in your life:

1. Confess and repent of all known sin.

2. Stop every doubtful habit or activity.

3. Immediately obey the Holy Spirit's prompting.

4. Publicly profess your faith in Christ.

5 Think about one family member, relative, coworker, or friend to whom you can tell the story of the revival in Wales. Invite them to pray with you that God will move in a transforming way in your community.

Pray that God will bend you in humility before Him. Pray that He will "Bend the church and save the world." Pray that the Lord of the harvest will thrust out laborers into the spiritual harvest fields of the world.

> *[Jesus] said to his disciples, "The harvest is plentiful, but the laborers are few; therefore pray earnestly to the Lord of the harvest to send out laborers into his harvest."*
> **Matthew 9:37-38** ✝

Evan Roberts
Sparked Revival in Wales (1904)

By the time he was 26, Evan Roberts had been praying for revival—in his own life and in his country—for more than a decade. Yet even in his diligence Evan recognized a hardness in his heart. Evan once heard someone pray, "Lord, bend us" and knew immediately that this was his need. The next night in a prayer meeting he knelt and cried out to the Lord, "Bend me! Bend me!"—and God did.

From that day forward Evan's life was ablaze with a love for God. He and his friends began asking God for 100,000 souls to come to salvation. On Monday night, October 31, 1904, Evans brought this four-point message to his home church at Loughor, Wales:

1. Is there any sin in your past that you have not confessed to God? On your knees at once. Your past must be put away and yourself cleansed.

2. Is there anything in your life that is doubtful—anything you cannot decide whether is good or evil? Away with it. There must not be a cloud between you and God.

3. Do what the Holy Spirit prompts you to do. Obey promptly, implicitly, and with unquestioning submission to God's Spirit.

4. Publicly profess Christ as your Savior.

His cry became "Bend the church and save the world." Once again God answered his prayer. As a matter of public record in 1904, sinful habits began to wane in Wales. Taverns closed, gambling businesses lost their trade, and brothels locked their doors. Families were reunited, broken friendships were reconciled, profanity ceased, old debts were paid, stolen goods were returned, and forgiveness for past offenses flowed. Divisions in churches were healed, denominational and class barriers were broken down, feuds were forgotten, and discord and enmity were replaced by peace and harmony and unity.

On that first night of Evan Roberts's preaching ministry, 16 young people confessed Christ. The next night 7 turned to Christ, and the third night 20 people received Jesus Christ as Lord. Attendance at meetings began to grow and spread to other towns and villages. The names of converts were sent to the newspapers. After two months 70,000 had come to Christ. By the end of March 1905, 85,000 and ultimately 100,000 confessed faith in Jesus Christ. God used this young man to change the spiritual course of an entire generation in Wales.[1]

---

1. "Bend the Church and Save the World," vol. 18, no. 1, Special Edition of *Spirit of Revival* (Buchanan, MI: Life Action Ministries).

downpour

Christ on the cross: a picture of grace

Christ on the cross:
a picture of grace
PART 1

key verse to memorize

*"Far be it from me to boast except in the cross
of our Lord Jesus Christ, by which the world
has been crucified to me, and I to the world."*

Galatians 6:14

For session 8 plans, turn to page 172 in the leader guide.

discussion guide on week 7: self in the dirt, part 2

1. Name and describe the five marks of genuine repentance.
2. Turn to page 96 and discuss the difference between godly grief (or sorrow) and worldly grief, using the statements in activity 1.
3. Which four words best help you understand the idea of repulsion toward sin (activity 2, p. 97)?
4. In activity 4 on page 98 responses 2 and 5 fall short of proper restitution. What would proper restitution look like in those instances?
5. Volunteers, share your experience of repentance and restitution. How have people responded to your appeals for forgiveness and reconciliation?
6. What were Evan Roberts's four points in the revival in Wales?
7. Take time to pray that God will change lives and begin transforming your community.

dvd session 8 message notes (27 minutes)

Scripture focus: Matthew 27:15-54
1. Christ on the _Substituting Cross_
   A. _Substitutionary_ (Matt. 27:15-23)
   B. _scandalizing_ (Matt. 27:24-44)
   C. _suffering_ (Matt. 27:45-50)
   D. _satisfying_ [the wrath of God] (Matt. 27:51-54)

Interview with worship leaders
- Going back to the cross for forgiveness (Matt)
- Deciding to walk with Christ, no turning back (Amy)
- Learning to trust Christ with my family and the things I love most (Matt)
- Giving up the things I love and receiving them back again (Josh)

snapshot summary

Jesus accomplished a significant work in our behalf by what He did on the cross substituting, scandalizing, suffering, and satisfying.

my goals for you

I want you to understand the significance of Christ's work on the cross for your spiritual benefit and to express your gratitude to Him for His great sacrifice.

- Giving up a dream for my future to trust Christ with the future (Lindsay)
- Trusting Christ when I faced a significant loss (Andi)

responding to the message

1. Can you identify with the testimony of one of the worship leaders? Which one and how? How has God been working in your life through the cross?
2. Review by answering the following questions.
   a. What four things did Jesus do on the cross? Briefly explain each one. What difference does that make for you today?
   b. Which aspect of Christ's work on the cross seems to be the most meaningful to you and why?
3. How have you seen the cross of Christ lifted up and/or ridiculed in the world around you?
4. Volunteers, pray sentence prayers thanking Christ for what He did for you on the cross.

preview statements for this week's study

- The cross of Jesus Christ is the signature symbol of the central event in the history of civilization.
- What's He doing there? Answer: He's subbing for you. He's taking God's wrath for *your* sin. He's satisfying the just demands of a holy God. He's paying the price that God's holiness requires so that you and I can be forgiven.
- The cross of Jesus Christ has always been irrationally and inexplicably an outrageous scandal.
- To have done nothing wrong and to be abandoned by God the Father— nothing compares to that kind of suffering.
- A holy God poured out His wrath on His innocent Son so that we could be forgiven.

Message-notes blanks: cross, Substituting, Scandalizing, Suffering, Satisfying

| # Jesus Is Substituting

The cross of Jesus Christ is the signature symbol of the central event in the history of civilization. Not until the second century was the cross welcomed as the central symbol of Christianity. In the fourth century the emperor Constantine saw it in a vision and banned it as an instrument of execution. In fact, the cross was never thought of as anything but a hideous instrument of death until everyone who had actually seen a crucifixion had died. Only then did people represent the cross as something sacred in sculpture, paintings, and other artistic forms.

Today we depict the cross as common. Jewelers pound it into all sorts of finery we can staple to our ears and wear around our necks. Merchandisers manufacture this symbol of unlimited atonement into fuzzy things for my rearview mirror or stand-ups for my garden. From teacups to T-shirts, the cross has cornered the market on crassness. Department stores hawk chocolate ones for Holy Week. Baseball players and businessmen cross themselves before a big moment. The cross itself has become big business. But it was never intended to be a lucky trinket. This is profanity in the truest sense. Is it any wonder we have lost the wonder of what happened on Calvary?

1 Think about your own spaces. Where do you find a cross? Check all that apply.
- ❏ On the mirror or back of my car
- ❏ On the front door of our house
- ❏ On a necklace around my neck
- ❏ On the desk in my office
- ❏ In our garden
- ❏ On clothing in my closet or drawers
- ❏ In our family/living room
- ❏ On the wall in a picture or painting
- ❏ On a shelf
- ❏ In the kitchen

2 Evaluate the use of the cross in your spaces above. How would you describe their value to you spiritually? Check one or write your own.
- ❏ a. They prompt me to think of Christ with love and reverence.
- ❏ b. They have become so commonplace that I don't pay much attention.
- ❏ c. I use them as a testimony of my love for Christ and faith in Him.
- ❏ d. I use them to prove to others how religious I am.
- ❏ e. Other: _____

_____

Christ's resurrection accomplished salvation and verified Christ's victory over death. But the cross of Jesus Christ showed us God's grace. Everything God wants us to know about Himself comes together in those crossbeams.

Our purpose this week is to elevate Christ's work on the cross. Think about Him there. In your mind's eye picture Jesus stretched out against the sky. What's He doing there? That's the question we will explore. We'll focus our attention on the Gospel of Matthew to discover four answers to that question: What's Jesus doing on the cross?
- He's substituting.
- He's scandalizing.
- He's suffering.
- He's satisfying.

downpour

He's Substituting

Picture Christ on the cross and ask yourself, *What's He doing there?* Answer: He's subbing for you. He's taking God's wrath for *your* sin. He's satisfying the just demands of a holy God. He's paying the price that God's holiness requires so that you and I can be forgiven.

Romans 6:23 says, "The wages of sin is death, but the free gift of God is eternal life in Christ Jesus our Lord." Second Corinthians 5:21 says, "For our sake [God] made him to be sin who knew no sin, so that in him we might become the righteousness of God."

What's Jesus doing on the cross? He's substituting: Jesus in my place. My heart overflows with gratitude when I think of Jesus Christ taking on Himself the penalty that was mine to bear! God demonstrated such love that "while we were still sinners, Christ died for us" (Rom. 5:8).

❸ What is one thing Jesus did for you on the cross?

_____

Jesus lived His life on earth at a time of revolution and unrest in the nation of Israel. The Romans had conquered and subjugated the land, and every day Hebrew insurgents battled in the streets. People didn't need TV; they watched drama right in front of them as their hometown boys were captured as resistance fighters and injured, killed, or carted off to prison—definitely the underdogs compared to the forces of Rome. You can imagine how the families and communities suffered in the aftershock of such conflict on a daily basis.

With that background we enter the story at the time of the Passover. This is Jewish culture's most celebrated time of year. The Jews were commanded by the Old Testament to remember the exodus from Egypt (see Ex. 12:43). The "Passover party" culminated in the Roman governor's releasing a prisoner of the people's choice to appease their anger and reduce their frustration with the Roman occupation. Matthew 27:15 reports that "at the feast the governor was accustomed to release for the crowd any one prisoner whom they wanted." This was Pilate's perfect opportunity to avert the murderous demands for Jesus' death by offering either Jesus or the most notorious prisoner called Barabbas. Pilate was trying to position Jesus as the favorite to be released. He said, "You choose. Do you want this mad revolutionary or Jesus?" He believed their sense of self-preservation would force them to choose Jesus. Verse 17 says, "When they had gathered, Pilate said to them, 'Whom do you want me to release for you: Barabbas, or Jesus who is called Christ?'"

In effect, Pilate was offering, "Do you want Osama bin Laden or Jesus? The BTK murderer or Jesus?" Surely they would want Jesus. Pilate knew that "it was out of envy that they had delivered him [Jesus] up." While Pilate "was sitting on the judgment seat, his wife sent word to him: 'Have nothing to do with that righteous man, for I have suffered much because of him today in a dream'" (vv. 18-19). Even Pilate's pagan wife was disturbed by the injustice being done to Christ. But, motivated by the religious leaders, the crowd was irrationally determined to see Christ die.

"Now the chief priests and the elders persuaded the crowd to ask for Barabbas and destroy Jesus." *Destroy*, a very strong word, actually means *annihilate him,* to erase not only His person but also the memory of His having ever lived. Wipe Him out so that He never existed. Verse 21 records the question again: "The governor again said to them, 'Which of the two do you want me to release for you?' And they said, 'Barabbas.' Pilate said to them, 'Then what shall I do with Jesus who is called Christ?' They all said, 'Let him be crucified!' Pilate was stunned, knowing that Barrabas was dangerous and Jesus was innocent. So he asked, "Why, what evil has he done?"

Everyone knew the evil Barabbas had done. Jesus was crucified between two robbers. Other translations say *thieves*. In the original language *robbers* doesn't refer to burglar types who comb neighborhoods looking for homes where the owners forgot to lock their patio doors. It literally means *revolutionaries*. The two men crucified on either side of Jesus were revolutionaries. Jesus died on the cross intended for Barabbas, the most notorious revolutionary, between two other revolutionaries. For that reason it is not stretching it at all to say that Jesus literally, physically took the cross that had been reserved for Barabbas. Jesus died in Barabbas's place.

4 **What do you think Barabbas felt at this strange turn of events? Check one.**
- ❏ a. Wow! What a lucky man I am!
- ❏ b. Wait! I can't believe what you're doing. You're executing an innocent man in my place? That's not right.
- ❏ c. Well! I deserved this break. It's about time the gods started showing me some favor.
- ❏ d. Other: _____

You can't understand the gospel until you understand this idea of substitution. Jesus died first for Barabbas and then for every other member of the human race who has ever lived. Barabbas is the first in the line, but behind him stands someone else and so on and so on. I am there in that line. You are too. Each of us deserves to die in payment for our own sin, but Jesus stepped in and took that penalty for us. I deserve to die that death, but the gift of God is eternal life through Jesus Christ. That's substitution. Jesus took my place on the cross. This is the central tenet of the historic gospel. That's good news!

5 **Draw three crosses below. Draw a stick figure of a person on each of the two outside crosses. Write above the one in the middle *My Cross*. Then meditate on the fact that Jesus took your place when He suffered and died on the cross.**

Tell Jesus what you are thinking and feeling at this strange turn of events: the perfect and innocent Son of God is taking your place. ✝

| # He's Scandalizing and Suffering

The cross is an outrageous offense. It doesn't matter at what vantage point you stand or where you grew up or what you know. The cross makes scandalous claims that cause intense reactions.

Pilate was so smug and self-assured that even the over-the-top, bloodthirsty crowd unsettled him. "So when Pilate saw that he was gaining nothing, but rather that a riot was beginning, he took water and washed his hands before the crowd, saying, 'I am innocent of this man's blood; see to it yourselves'" (Matt. 27:24).

The Jews rejecting Christ called out for His crucifixion. Crucifixion was the most shameful, painful, awful death a person could experience, and they wanted it for Jesus. They passionately pleaded for Christ's torturous death in a way that defies explanation.

① **Underline the words describing ways people scandalously mistreated the Lord. I've underlined one for you.**

"The soldiers of the governor took Jesus into the governor's headquarters, and they gathered the whole battalion [600 soldiers] *before him. And <u>they stripped him</u> and put a scarlet robe on him, and twisting together a crown of thorns, they put it on his head and put a reed in his right hand. And kneeling before him, they mocked him* [meaning they made him look like a fool], *... And they spit on him ... And when they had mocked him, they stripped him of the robe ... and led him away to crucify him. ...*

"They offered him wine to drink, mixed with gall [a narcotic to dull the pain], *but when he tasted it, he would not drink it. ... Those who passed by derided him, wagging their heads and saying, ... 'He saved others; he cannot save himself.' ... And the robbers who were crucified with him also reviled him in the same way."*

Matthew 27:27-44

First the Romans, then the Jewish leaders, now even the criminals take their shot at the Savior on the cross. What a scandal! A scandal is an action or event that causes a public outcry and generates expressions of malicious sentiment. The cross of Jesus Christ has always been irrationally and inexplicably an outrageous scandal.

It goes on to this day everywhere around us. You can follow Mohammed or Ghandi or any religion of the East. You can be a washed-out liberal Christian or a closet Catholic, and everything will be wonderful. You can be for abortion, promote homosexuality, and support every liberal agenda in the country, and polite company will, at worst, smile with deference. Not until someone whose heart is in the grip of this world finds out that you have given your heart to Jesus Christ and that He is the greatest treasure of your heart will you begin to experience intense hatred and irrational behavior.

② Briefly describe one or more times you have observed hatred or irrational behavior directed at Jesus Christ or His followers.

_____

_____

_____

A battle rages as Satan and his demonic army spend themselves to incite hatred against the cross of Jesus Christ. Very few are neutral in this battle; most are firmly entrenched and fighting on one side or the other. When you live for Christ and express to others the message of the cross, you will experience this scandalizing hatred.

What's Jesus doing on that cross? He's fighting for the souls of men. He's seeking to redeem them from their own scandalizing hatred. Hear the soldiers laughing and mocking as the Savior gives up His life for them. Two thousand years later, people still scream and mock the cross of Jesus. It's a scandal!

⟩ Pause and thank Jesus for enduring the scandalizing treatment for you.

Jesus Is Suffering

"When they had crucified him …" (Matt. 27:35). Who can come close to detailing all this phrase means? Isaiah 52:14 tells us that Jesus' "appearance was so marred" that he didn't look like a man. These historical realities are more firmly fixed in our mind's eye since the release of the movie _The Passion of the Christ_. As brutal as it was to watch, it doesn't come close to capturing Jesus' excruciating suffering on the cross.

The physical pain, however, was the lesser issue in Jesus' suffering. "From the sixth hour there was darkness over all the land until the ninth hour. And about the ninth hour Jesus cried out with a loud voice, saying, … "My God, my God, why have you forsaken me?' " (Matt. 27:45-46). From eternity past Jesus had known only perfect unity with His Father. Now as He hung on the cross, He experienced total separation from that perfect unity. What finite mind can comprehend separating the inseparable? Forsaken by the Father? A love that was infinitely deep, eternal, and everlasting was lost in that darkness.

It would be one thing if Jesus had simply been separated from the dark-hearted, pagan people screaming insults at Him and headed for hell themselves. Abandonment by pagans meant nothing. It's still another thing for Jesus to be abandoned by the weak-willed disciples who were following at a distance anyway. Certainly there was pain in that, but He had a realistic understanding of their weakness. But to have done nothing wrong and to be abandoned by God the Father—nothing compares to that kind of suffering. That is the suffering of the cross.

3 **"The wages of sin is death" (Rom. 6:23). How much did Jesus suffer because of your sin? Check one.**

❑ a. My sin was sufficient to cause the Father to forsake Him. I caused His emotional agony of being abandoned by His Father.

❑ b. My sin debt is big enough that it required death. I caused His physical agony, including death.

❑ c. Both a and b.

❑ d. Not much. I've been a pretty good person. Surely very little of His suffering was my doing.

Did you check c? His physical death and abandonment by the Father were both necessary to pay the death penalty for any one of us. If you checked d, you haven't seen your sin in the mirror very clearly. Jesus had to die for you.

In your Bible read Isaiah 53 and pause to pray after each verse or two. Thank Jesus for the specific suffering He endured for you. ☦

day 3 | Jesus Is Satisfying

If the cross of Jesus Christ is the central target at which all biblical content shoots, the subject of how His death satisfies God's wrath is the bull's-eye. The gospel of Jesus Christ is only a concept until we comprehend the way Jesus' death on the cross satisfied God's wrath for sin.

Matthew 27:51 reports, "Behold, the curtain of the temple was torn in two, from top to bottom. And the earth shook, and the rocks were split." The temple represented God's presence. God dwelled in unapproachable holiness at the back of the temple in the holy of holies behind an impenetrable curtain. No one went into the holy of holies behind the curtain, which was at least eight inches thick, except a priest and then only once a year. The curtain reminded everyone of the sin that separated man and God.

How awesome to read in Matthew 27:50–51 that at the precise moment, when Jesus "cried out again with a loud voice and yielded up his spirit," immediately "the curtain of the temple was torn in two, *from top to bottom*" (emphasis added). The temple curtain had kept people out of God's presence, but at the moment Jesus died as an atoning sacrifice for sin, the veil was torn in two, not from bottom to top as if a man were standing there saying, "We don't need this anymore" but from top to bottom because God Himself reached down and tore the symbol of His separation from each of us. Because Jesus suffered and was substituted for us, He satisfied the wrath of a holy God against sin. Now the way is open to God. Sin is now paid for. "The way is open," He declares. "Come into My presence. Wrath is averted. My Son has paid the price for your sin. Evil, sinful men can now approach holiness." Why? Because of the cross. With this action of tearing the temple veil, God says, "Sin has been paid for. Satisfied!" *paid in full*

1 Your sin debt—a debt you could never repay—has been paid for by Jesus! Write over the top of the words below "Paid in Full."

MY SIN DEBT

God wanted us to know that something had changed for all time. Not only was the curtain torn, but God Himself also reached down and shook the earth and said, "I want people to know something is happening—pay attention!" Look at this: "The tombs also were opened. And many bodies of the saints who had fallen asleep were raised, and coming out of the tombs after his resurrection they went into the holy city and appeared to many" (Matt. 27:52-53). A sign from heaven said, "Pay attention. Something big is happening here." It's unparalleled. It's unprecedented. Nothing like this will ever happen again.

God is satisfied in the cross of Jesus Christ. So awesome and obviously supernatural was all this that Scripture records, "When the centurion and those who were with him, keeping watch over Jesus, saw the earthquake and what took place, they were filled with awe and said, 'Truly this was the Son of God!' " (v. 54).

I wonder if we can imagine just how much God hates sin. God hates sin with an infinite loathing we can't comprehend. Think of every act of cruel barbarism that twists your stomach into a knot. Think of every act of perversity measured out against pure innocence by rampant, heartless perversion. Think of the sickening things happening in this moment that no one knows about except God. Also in this moment, at this very second, the totality of that wickedness rises as it always has and will, as an unceasing stench to the nostrils of God.

Some people ask, "Why doesn't God do something about sin?" News flash: He did. All God's righteous hatred of all that sin from all of human history was poured out on Christ as He hung there on that cross. On Him almighty judgment fell that would have sunk the world to hell.

A holy God poured out His wrath on His innocent Son so that we could be forgiven. When Jesus said, "It is finished," God said, "Paid in full." Sin has been put away now. In a way we will never fully comprehend, the cross of Jesus Christ satisfied the requirements of a holy God.

2 Write a verse of a poem or song that describes "Debt Satisfied" or "Paid in Full." If you prefer, write a prayer of gratitude to the Lord.

at the cross

Thank God for what Jesus did on the cross for you as He substituted, scandalized, suffered, and satisfied. ✝

| # Nail It to the Cross

Activate

God now wants to take the sins you've repented of by His grace and nail them to the cross of Christ. They aren't your problem anymore. Colossians 2:14 is very clear: the debt is canceled; the sin is nailed to the cross.

> *"You, who were dead in your trespasses ... God made alive together with him, having forgiven us all our trespasses, by canceling the record of debt that stood against us with its legal demands. This he set aside, nailing it to the cross."*
> **Colossians 2:13-14**

1 **Review your list(s) of the sins that God has shown you (see pp. 67 and 81 and/or your journal). Answer the following questions for each one. You do not need to check responses below.**

1. Do you see this sin for what it is? Do you feel the weight of it?
   ❏ Yes, I'm certain. ❏ I'm beginning to. ❏ No ❏ No response

2. Have you confessed it to the Lord and asked for forgiveness?
   ❏ Yes, I'm certain. ❏ I think so. ❏ No ❏ No response

3. Have you repented of it and made any necessary restitution?
   ❏ Yes, I'm certain. ❏ I think so. ❏ Not yet ❏ No response

2 **Select a tangible symbol that could help you remember that your sin is now surrendered to God and forgiven. Choose one below or one of your own. Keep it in a place where you can be reminded over the next few weeks that your sin debt has been paid by Christ.**

❏ a. A red dot or drop of red fingernail polish on the face of your watch
❏ b. A small cross in your pocket or in your purse (Although the use of the cross can become crass, filling your use of it with meaning is different.)
❏ c. A red bracelet, ring, or other object to wear
❏ d. A blunted nail
❏ e. Other: _____

The next time you are tempted to choose that sin again or if Satan whispers that God's forgiveness couldn't cover it, remind yourself that Christ's blood cleanses you from that sin and you now have power over it. You are dead to sin and alive to Christ.

Worship God in Spirit and Truth

We have pondered together God's great grace in sending Jesus to die in our place. The next best thing we can do now is worship Him.

❸ Read or sing "When I Survey the Wondrous Cross" by Isaac Watts. As you read the verses, underline things you can do in response to the cross.

> When I survey the wondrous cross
> On which the Prince of glory died,
> My richest gain I count but loss,
> And pour contempt on all my pride.
>
> Forbid it, Lord, that I should boast,
> Save in the death of Christ my God!
> All the vain things that charm me most,
> I sacrifice them to His blood.
>
> See from His head, His hands, His feet,
> Sorrow and love flow mingled down!
> Did e'er such love and sorrow meet,
> Or thorns compose so rich a crown?
>
> Were the whole realm of nature mine,
> That were a present far too small;
> Love so amazing, so divine,
> Demands my soul, my life, my all.

You can count human gains as loss and pour contempt on your pride. You can give up the vain things that charm you most. You can give Him your love, your soul, your life, and your all.

❹ What will you do in response to the grace and provision of the cross?

_____

❺ Use a hymnal or go online to *www.cyberhymnal.org* and read or sing hymns about the cross and grace as guides for your worship.

❭ Elevate
Take time to thank the Lord for grace and the cross. Use this prayer and other words of your own.

Lord, thank You for the picture of Your grace in the cross of Your dear Son. How great is Your love for Your children—and that includes me. How unceasing. How unending. How unparalleled. How unprecedented. Where could I ever find such grace that my heart so desperately needs?

Lord, thank You that my failures of the past are nailed to the cross. You have canceled the debt that is against me from everything about which I feel secretly ashamed. The enemy would say that my best days are behind me. But You say that I still have an opportunity to be the man or woman of righteousness that I am now becoming in You. There's still time. Today is a new beginning for me. Today I start in grace. How could I continue in sin now that I know what it cost You? Thank You for Your presence here and now. I draw near to You. In Jesus' name. Amen.

downpour

day 5 | Peter's Personal Revival

1 Read about the picture of personal revival from the life of Peter on page 118 and read the biblical accounts of his sin and restoration in Luke 22:31-34,54-62 and John 21.

———————

2 Jesus warned Peter of his impending test of faith and predicted his denial. What do you think Peter felt as he bitterly wept following his failure? Check a response or write your own.

❏ a. He focused on self: "I claimed to be ready to die with Him. Whom am I kidding? I'm a a coward. My whole life is a sham. I'm ashamed and embarrassed by my actions."

❏ b. He focused on Christ: "He must have been so hurt by my denials. I was one of his closest friends, but I turned my back on Him when He was in such need. I can't believe I added to His suffering. His suffering was great enough without my adding to it."

❏ c. Other: _a + b_ _____

_____

3 Can you recall a time when you wept because of your sin and spiritual failure? If so, where was your focus? Check one or write your own.

❏ a. I focused on myself, my weakness, and my wickedness.

❏ b. I focused more on how I must have shamed and wounded Christ.

❏ c. I was hurt realizing that my relationship with God was broken.

❏ d. I was more hurt because others knew of my sin and my Christian witness and reputation were severely damaged.

❏ e. Other: _____

_____

4 What do you think Peter felt after Jesus's talk by the lake? Check one.

❏ a. Fearful at the prospect of painful and sacrificial service to Him

❏ b. A renewed challenge to love and follow Christ and serve His people

❏ c. Sweet forgiveness, love, and acceptance

You've confessed all of your sins to Christ and sought to repent. Now Jesus asks, "Do you love Me?" Talk to Jesus about your renewed love for Him. Express your gratitude for His loving sacrifice and for the forgiveness granted. Now hear Him say to you, "Follow Me." ✝

From the Life of Peter: A Picture of God's Grace

LUKE 22:31-34,54-62; JOHN 21

To Peter that moment by the fire in Caiaphas's courtyard marked the greatest crisis of his life. He must have relived the scene over and over again, wishing to snatch back his words "I do not know Him!" He had spit out that denial not once but three times. Somewhere in the night a rooster stretched its neck and punctuated his faith's failure. In that horrid moment Peter looked over his shoulder and caught the eye of the One who loved him more than life, passing through the courtyard on His way to the cross. That moment between sinner and Savior must have hung in the air like a framed picture.

Peter turned his face from the fire and wept. What burned more? The fire's acrid smoke that blew into his eyes or the conviction of the sin that pierced his heart?

Wasn't it earlier that same night Peter had vowed, "Others will turn away, Lord, but I won't"?

Go ahead and be hard on Peter. Talk about how impulsive he was or how he shot off his mouth. He probably heard the rebuke all the time. But something happened that changed Peter between that devastating moment by this fire and the time when he stood with the Lord by another fire several mornings later.

In those days in between, Peter's guilt could have driven him to the cynical edge: *What was I thinking to believe He was the Christ anyway?* He could have run, never to return. His heart could have become hardened with unbelief. For sure, if you don't deal with your sin, it can drive you to some awful places.

But that's not the Peter we meet three days later rushing into Jesus' empty tomb (see John 20:3-9), or the Peter who throws himself into the lake to get to Jesus (see John 21:7-9), or the Peter Jesus pulls aside in private conversation and restores to friendship and ministry (see John 21:15-17). Did they speak of that awful moment by the fire? We don't know; that's between them. We do know that Peter's crisis had taken him to the right place with God. Sin, rightly understood, prompted repentance. And repentance had turned him around to meet the face of grace.

This, then, is revival. Peter recognized his sin. He rightly understood his problem. He turned away from his sin and to the Lord, and then the grace made possible by Jesus Christ's ransom on the cross released him from sin's power. Peter returned to the Lord with a whole heart—stronger, more humble, ready for greater days ahead. That's revival. ✝

Christ on the cross: a picture of grace

PART 2

Christ on the cross: a picture of grace

PART 2

key verse to memorize

"He has delivered us from the domain of darkness
and transferred us to the kingdom of his beloved Son,
in whom we have redemption, the forgiveness of sins."
Colossians 1:13-14

For session 9 plans, turn to page 173 in the leader guide.

discussion guide on week 8: Christ on the cross, part 1

1. What was Jesus doing on the cross?
2. Share your responses to activities 1 and 2 on page 108.
3. What do you think Barabbas felt when Jesus took his place on the center cross (activity 4, p. 110)?
4. How have you observed Jesus Christ, His followers, and the cross being scandalized by the words and actions of others (see activity 2, p. 112)?
5. What are some ways Jesus suffered on the day He was crucified?
6. Volunteers, share the symbol you selected to remind you that Christ has paid your sin debt (activity 2, p. 115).
7. Discuss your responses to the activities on page 117 about Peter's revival.

dvd session 9 message notes (28 minutes)

1. Christ on the cross (last week's topic)
2. A picture of Grace
   A. Grace that *redeems*
      Penalty *Gone* (Col. 1:13-14)
      • Apart from Christ you would be in the kingdom of darkness.
      • Christ paid a price to get us back.
   B. Grace that *Releases*
      Power *Broken* (Rom. 6:14)
      • You can choose what is right.
      • You can please God.
   C. Grace that *reconciles*
      Prejudice *Killed* (Eph. 2:14-15)
      • Prejudice is great wickedness.
      • Every follower of Jesus ought to hate it with holy indignation.

snapshot summary

Christ on the cross is God's picture of grace that redeems, releases, reconciles, and removes. The penalty and power of sin are gone.

my goals for you

I want you to understand God's amazing grace for you and show your joy by explaining God's grace to someone else.

D. Grace that _removes_
   Past _____ _gone_ _____ (Col. 2:13-14)
   • God says to every person deformed by sin, "I wish you were Mine."

Message music: see the "Sea of Grace" lyrics on page 122.

responding to the message

1. Review the lyrics of "Sea of Grace" and read Micah 7:18-19 on page 122. What has God done with our sins?
2. Review by answering the following questions.
   a. Apart from Christ's grace where would we be?
   b. What are four things Christ's grace has done for you? What difference does each one make?
   c. What difference does Christ's grace make in your relationships with people who are different from you?
   d. What has Christ done with your past sins?
3. Volunteers, pray sentence prayers of thanksgiving for the many ways you have experienced His grace. Be specific in your thanks.

preview statements for this week's study

• God doesn't give paychecks; God gives grace. Unearned, undeserved, unmerited—that's grace.
• Grace is the oxygen of Christian living once we have dealt with sin God's way through personal repentance.
• Christ on the cross is the 3-D, Technicolor, IMAX, to-the-max, living picture of God's grace—grace to redeem us from the penalty of sin, release us from the power of sin, reconcile us to one another, and remove the shame of our past.

Message-notes blanks: redeems, gone, releases, broken, reconciles, gone, removes, gone

Sea of Grace

have compassion on me God, / and hear my desperate cry
i've turned away from truth, / and followed after lies
so i'm waiting for You here, / i'm longing for Your mercy
draw me back to You, / restore my soul completely

for who God is like You? You pardon my sin
You love to show mercy, show mercy again
and take all my sin, take all my shame
and throw them into Your never ending sea
sea of grace

i know You're listening / i know You hear my cry,
so i put my hope in You / though i've fallen, i will rise
and then i will sing / and tell of Your great mercy
that restored and rescued me / from darkness into light

"Who is a God like you, pardoning iniquity and passing over transgression for the remnant of his inheritance? He does not retain his anger forever, because he delights in steadfast love. He will again have compassion on us; he will tread our iniquities under foot. You will cast all our sins into the depths of the sea."
Micah 7:18-19

Slowly read the lyrics above and meditate on the meaning of this song. Use the following activities to apply this message to your life.
1. Think about and praise God for His compassion and mercy in hearing your cry and forgiving your sin.
2. Think about the sins you have confessed to the Lord in recent weeks and imagine them disappearing in the depths of the sea!

Thank God for the completeness of His forgiveness and for His forgetfulness about forgiven sin. Use the lines below to describe His great mercy.

_____

_____

Note: "Sea of Grace" is recorded for you on the DVDs, but it is not on the Message-Music CD.

downpour

| # Grace That Redeems

Four Pictures of Grace

Because God gave Jesus the penalty for our sin while He hung on the cross, God can give us something else, something we don't deserve—grace. Everything we have ever received from God is because of grace. God doesn't give paychecks; God gives grace. Unearned, undeserved, unmerited—that's grace.

❶ Which of the following words do *not* belong with grace? Check all that apply.

❏ costly to Christ	❏ costly to you	❏ deserved
❏ earned	❏ freely given	❏ gift
❏ undeserved	❏ unearned	❏ wages

Grace was costly to Christ but not to you. You can't earn it, deserve it, or demand it as wages. Undeserved and unearned, it is a gift of God, freely given. To understand and embrace the impact of grace in your life, let's review passages of Scripture that teach us what grace is and what grace does.

Grace That Redeems—The Penalty Is Gone

Apart from Christ we belong to the kingdom of darkness, but because of grace, our penalty is gone:

> *"He* [the Father] *has delivered us from the domain of darkness*
> *and transferred us to the kingdom of his beloved Son,*
> *in whom we have redemption, the forgiveness of sins."*
> **Colossians 1:13-14**

Where would you be today apart from God's grace? You would be in the kingdom of darkness. If you have the privilege of knowing Jesus Christ personally through faith in Him, exactly how did you get that relationship? Did God look down and say, "You're better than average. I think I'll take you." Is that how it happened? No. There was nothing special about you or me or anyone who has received His grace. Nothing about us drew God to us. He extended His grace to us freely.

God chose to set His love on you. He reached down and took hold of you—and looking back, you realize that you couldn't have even resisted Him. He came after you. He conquered your will. He drew you to Himself. He loves You. That's grace.

Apart from Christ our citizenship is in hell. There is no way out. The storm of His wrath was coming on you like the urban poor of New Orleans just before Hurricane Katrina. We were trapped with no way out, and the waters of God's wrath were rising until Christ stepped in and led our souls to higher ground. Without that grace we would have drowned.

Verse 14 says, "We have redemption, the forgiveness of sin." That pictures Christ's death as payment to God. He didn't just come and get us; He paid a price to get us back. Do you know what it means to be forgiven of your sin? It means that no wrong you've ever done can be held against you. Think of all the sin lingering in your imperfect memory of the past. In Christ it cannot be held against you. It's unbelievable! In Him we have redemption through His blood. We have the forgiveness of sins. Can you even take it in? We have been spared the horror of God's wrath in hell. As Satan and his demonic host are heading for an eternal home in the lake of fire, they will notice that a few of us are gone ... because of God's grace.

2 **Who paid the price for your redemption?** _____

3 **Because of the grace purchased by Christ's blood, what has been done with the penalty of your sin? The penalty is** _____

Apart from Christ we are bankrupt, with nothing to offer in payment. That is the condition of every person in the world—bankrupt, with no capacity to pay, nothing with which to appease the wrath of a holy God. What in your life could satisfy God's demand for perfection? Nothing. Only God can. When we are bankrupt, not able to satisfy God's demands, God Himself steps in and pays the price for us. That's redemption. Because of grace the penalty of your sin is gone. It's outrageous! As the hymn proclaims, "Marvelous grace of our loving Lord, freely bestowed on all who believe; ... Grace that is greater than all my sin." [1] No wonder we call it amazing grace.

Take time to reflect on all your sin from which grace redeemed you. Thank God that the penalty is gone. Thank Jesus for paying the price.

---

1. Julia H. Johnston, "Grace Greater than Our Sin."

day 2 | Grace That Releases and Grace That Reconciles

Grace That Releases—The Power Is Broken

Grace redeems, but that's not all! If you know only the grace that redeems and not the grace that releases, you're like an astronaut, all strapped in the space shuttle but still on the launch pad. Or you're like a mountain climber at base camp.

The best stuff is up ahead! So many of Jesus' followers settle for just the fire insurance. They experience the forgiveness from the penalty of sin but not release from the power of sin in their lives going forward. I've got phenomenal news: there's more to this grace than simply a home in heaven. Grace also releases you from the power of sin here and now. Do you want more of that?

1 **Have you experienced grace that releases from the power of sin? Check one or write your own.**

❏ a. So far I've settled for "fire insurance" to keep me out of hell. I'm redeemed, but you're telling me there's more?

❏ b. I've tasted grace that breaks the power of sin in my life. But I have to confess that some strongholds still need to be broken.

❏ c. I left base camp a while back. I'm pressing on to higher ground. I'm experiencing freedom from sin's dominion. Praise the Lord!

❏ d. Other: _____

_____

To the fire-insturance folks, yes, there's more! Isn't that good news?

> *"Sin will have no dominion over you,*
> *since you are not under law but under grace."*
> **Romans 6:14**

All the law can do is make you feel like a failure. But you're not under the law anymore; sin doesn't have to have dominion over you. The word *dominion* is both official and functional authority—as in, not just the police at your door but the police at your door with a gun to your head and your hands behind your back. That's the way sin had dominion over me before I came to Christ. Sin would say, "Jump," and I would say, "How high?" Now sin says, "Jump," and I say, "Get lost! You're not in charge anymore. I don't have to do what you say. I'm under grace now. My life belongs to Christ, and I want to do what He wants me to do." You have freedom to choose what is right. You can please God. You can live a life of righteousness. Grace makes personal, experiential righteousness possible.

You say, "Righteousness is the last word I would use to describe my experience this past week." Hey, get up! God loves you. Christ declares you righteous because of your personal faith in Him. You can begin again. The power of sin is broken. The choice is yours. Embrace that truth and live in it.

Experience the grace that releases. John 8:36 says, "If the Son sets you free, you will be free indeed." That's the power of the gospel. If you have only grace that redeems and not grace that releases, you're still at base camp. So much more is up ahead for you. Let God give it to you.

You're under grace. It doesn't matter what Satan says to you. It doesn't matter what your past says about you. It doesn't matter what unloving people say about you. Here's what God says about you: you're under His grace. Grace is what He sees; grace is what He knows. Grace is the oxygen of Christian living once we have dealt with sin God's way through personal repentance.

That's reason to pray. Thank the Lord and choose to live in victory.

Grace That Reconciles—The Prejudice Is Gone

Prejudice is prominent all over the world. People who are different have a tendency to avoid, use, abuse, mistreat, misunderstand, slander, accuse, fight, blame, and even kill people who are different. That's our sinful human nature.

2 What kinds of prejudice have you experienced or observed firsthand? Check all that apply.
- ❏ Racial prejudice (like black vs. white)
- ❏ Ethnic prejudice (like Japanese vs. Chinese)
- ❏ Economic prejudice (like rich vs. poor)
- ❏ Educational prejudice (like educated vs. illiterate)
- ❏ National prejudice (like English vs. French)
- ❏ Regional prejudice (like Yankees vs. Southerners)
- ❏ Political prejudice (like Democrats vs. Republicans)
- ❏ Generational prejudice (like Boomers vs. Gen Xers)
- ❏ Denominational prejudice (like Baptists vs. Presbyterians)

What other prejudices have you experienced or observed?

_____

_____

The list of prejudices could go on for pages. Ours isn't the first century with racial and social unrest. In Paul's day fierce tension raged between Jews and Gentiles, even within the walls of the early church.

> *"He himself is our peace, who has made us both one and has broken down in his flesh the dividing wall of hostility by abolishing the law of commandments and ordinances, that he might create in himself one new man in place of the two, so making peace."*
> **Ephesians 2:14-15**

Paul writes that Jesus has broken down in his flesh the dividing wall of hostility. By allowing Himself to be crucified as a substitute for our sin, Jesus broke down the barriers that separate us from one another. That's not only a better relationship with God but also a new heart for others, especially those who, humanly speaking, would be harder for you to love. God's grace causes us to seek reconciliation with people in every race, class, and culture. That's why the church of Jesus Christ should be the most diverse place in all of society. Christ has broken down the walls that separate us. Grace reconciles us—it makes us one. People who don't normally get together do so at the cross of Jesus Christ.

I live in Chicago, and *hostility* best describes the relationship between people all around us. Too often the focus is on what divides us—different races, different social classes, different backgrounds. "You're not like me," we say. "I don't know you." God forgive us. God intends grace to sweep all that darkness out of our hearts "that he might create in himself one new man in place of the two, so making peace, and might reconcile us both to God in one body through the cross, thereby killing the hostility" (Eph. 2:15-16). Do you know what that means? Not just right with God but right with others.

When you come to know Jesus Christ by faith and experience God's grace, you get a love for people as you've never known. You encounter people different from you, and you find yourself trying to bridge that separation. That's grace alive in you. You meet people who are educationally different from you, and you love them. You observe people who are culturally different from you, and you love them. You get with people who are racially different from you, and you love them.

3 **Review the list of prejudices in activity 2 on the opposite page. Would you have to confess that you have some of those prejudices in your mind and heart? If so, write the people or groups below.**

_____

_____

_____

Confess to the Lord your need for His grace, which removes prejudice and produces oneness and unity. Give Him permission to give you a new heart for the people He has chosen to love.

It takes a lot of courage and faith to come to a church where you are not the majority. In our church I frequently embrace and publicly thank the so-called minorities (we are all minorities somewhere in the world) who choose to worship with us. They are enriching the worship and the glory that goes to Jesus Christ, because what they are really saying is, "I belong with people who belong with Jesus even though they're different from me in many other ways." That kind of effort takes courage and reflects God's grace. Together we are saying, "Even if we look different, even if our backgrounds are different, whatever is different, this is the same—we love and follow Jesus Christ." That's what the cross of Jesus does—it reconciles people.

If you've experienced God's grace, you ought to hate prejudice. Every follower of Jesus Christ—whatever your race, denomination, or social background—ought to hate prejudice of every kind with holy indignation. If you've experienced the grace of the cross of Christ, something in you should repudiate unfounded, overgeneralized, stereotyped thinking that has formed without a solid assessment of the facts. All those who have been redeemed are one in Christ. That's the power of grace—it reconciles.

Respond to the Lord in prayer. Thank Him for grace that reconciles people and removes prejudice. Ask for that grace to work in areas where your old patterns need to be changed. Pray for victory over this sin too. ↑

Grace That Removes

Grace That Removes—My Past Is Gone

You might say, "My issue is not the way I see those who are different from me. My issue is the way I see myself. My problem is the choices I have made and the things I have done. When I think of living in God's grace, the biggest barrier is what I see in me." Do you realize that the entire body of Christ is made up of people like you? We have all experienced grace because we have all come to understand that we really needed it. Notice this:

> *"You, who were dead in your trespasses, ... God made alive together with him, having forgiven us all our trespasses, by canceling the record of debt that stood against us"*
> **Colossians 2:13-14**

Grace asserts that all past sins are wiped away because of the cross.

- How can a murderous revolutionary who died for his actions receive the promise of eternal paradise just because he comes around at the last minute (see Luke 23:42-43)? It's called grace.
- Why would a man stoop to help his sworn enemy who had been robbed and beaten (the religious dudes all took a pass) and then spend his resources to restore his enemy's health and strength (see Luke 10:33-35)? It's called grace.
- How can a guy who shows up for the last part of the workday get the exact same pay as others who have been slaving for hours in the hot sun (see Matt. 20:8-15)? It's called grace.
- Why does the son who lived like a pig and then moved in with the pigs get to be forgiven, restored, and have a party thrown in his honor (see Luke 15:11-31)? It's called grace.

A list of amazing-grace stories in the New Testament could fill many pages. Each one is shocking, outrageous, unearned, and undeserved. It's called grace!

1 **Is this an area where you still struggle to accept God's truth about your past? Check one.**
   - ❏ a. No. Thank God, my past is gone. Sure, I still remember it, but it doesn't affect my day-to-day walk with the Lord.
   - ❏ b. Yes. I know what you're saying in my head, but my heart isn't willing to let it go. And even my mind at times tries to convince me against what I know is true.
   - ❏ c. I'd answer both yes and no. Sometimes I seem to walk in freedom from my past, and other times I'm in the middle of my shame.

Where Is My Past Now?

Believe me when I tell you that God does not want His children wallowing in a past He has forgiven. If you're wondering what happened to all the wrong you so deeply regret, hear it now again: God canceled "the record of debt that stood against us with its legal demands. This he set aside, nailing it to the cross" (Col. 2:14).

Sometimes the greatest barrier is the way we see ourselves. We won't live in the grace that God proclaims over us. We won't embrace and experience the immense freedom that true grace gives. Maybe you don't feel worthy of God's love. Maybe you're ashamed of where you've been and what you've done. You wonder if you could ever feel clean again. Sin is not a trifle; if you've been carefully reading and doing the exercises in these pages, you know that very well by now. Holiness is God's standard, and when we really comprehend what that means, we are overwhelmed by the sin we see in the mirror. Real repentance from that sin finally brings us in exhaustion to the place where grace has been waiting all along. Not until we fully grasp the gravity of our sin problem can we grasp the amazing solution that God has provided by grace. Christ on the cross is the 3-D, Technicolor, IMAX, to-the-max, living picture of God's grace—grace to redeem us from the penalty of sin, release us from the power of sin, reconcile us with one another, and remove the shame of our past.

Pray and ask the Lord to enable you to believe Him rather than yourself. Read again the lyrics of "Sea of Grace" (p. 122) as part of your prayer.

Match the description of what grace does on the left with the results it produces on the right. Write a letter beside each number.

___ 1. Grace redeems.	a. My prejudice is gone.
___ 2. Grace releases.	b. My past is gone.
___ 3. Grace reconciles.	c. The power of sin is broken.
___ 4. Grace removes.	d. The penalty is gone.

(Answers: 1–d, 2–c, 3–a, 4–b)

Now match each description of grace above with a Scripture below that helps paint that picture of grace. Write a number from the list above beside each Scripture below.

___ "Sin will have no dominion over you, since you are not under law but under grace" (Rom. 6:14).

___ "He himself is our peace, who has made us both one and has broken down in his flesh the dividing wall of hostility by abolishing the law of commandments and ordinances, that he might create in himself one new man in place of the two, so making peace" (Eph. 2:14-15).

___ "He has delivered us from the domain of darkness and transferred us to the kingdom of his beloved Son, in whom we have redemption, the forgiveness of sins" (Col. 1:13-14).

___ "You, who were dead in your trespasses and the uncircumcision of your flesh, God made alive together with him, having forgiven us all our trespasses, by canceling the record of debt that stood against us with its legal demands. This he set aside, nailing it to the cross" (Col. 2:13-14).

(Answers: 2, 3, 1, 4)

Thank God for grace! Confess (agree with God about) the truths in the Scriptures above. Receive all the grace He's ready to give. ↑

| # Painting a Picture of Grace

Replicate

The great thing about grace is that it's meant to be shared. Can you paint for another person a picture of the grace you have experienced?

❶ Read the following suggestions about ways you can paint a picture of grace by telling someone about what Christ has done in your life. Select one or more and glorify your Lord by telling someone the good news about Christ's grace. Draw a star beside the one(s) you plan to use.

1. Grace That Redeems—The Penalty Is Gone

Ask yourself, *Where would I be today apart from God's grace? What future would I have to look forward to in this life and in eternity?* Tell someone about how far you've come—by grace. Compare what life was like for you B.C. (before Christ) with what it is like today. Share Colossians 2:13-14 with them and tell what the verses mean to you.

2. Grace That Releases—The Power Is Gone

Ask yourself, *How have my choices changed under grace? Do I choose to live under sin's control, or am I experiencing God's power to say no? Am I living as free as I am?* Tell someone about ways your choices have changed since you've come to Christ or even as recently as you've begun this study. Describe for them what your preference used to be and, by the grace of God, how that desire has changed. Read Romans 6:13-14 and explain how the Spirit of Jesus living in you can help you be free from the dominion of sin.

3. Grace That Reconciles—The Prejudice Is Gone

Ask yourself, *Whom have I stiff-armed, either in attitude or action? Do I need to ask God's forgiveness for my arrogance in thinking I'm better than they are? Am I willing for God to bring someone different from me up close and personal? Do I hate prejudice as much as I should?* Show God's grace to someone who used to be an object of your prejudice. Create an opportunity to get to know them. Cultivate a relationship with them. Ask them how you can pray for them—and then pray for them and even with them.

4. Grace That Removes—The Past Is Gone

Ask yourself, *am I still dragging around anything from my past with me? Have I asked God to forgive me for it? Have I repented of it? Then what is my problem?* Give it to God and get on with life. Someone you know thinks God could never forgive him of things in his past. Ask God for the discernment and the words in leading that person to God's grace, whether he has not yet received Christ's offer of salvation or is a struggling Christian. Tell him about God's "sea of grace."

Pray that the Lord will give you courage and love to share His grace with _____ (name). Pray that he or she will respond to His grace too. ✝

day 5 | Personal Revival Among the Moravian Brethren

1 Read about the picture of personal revival for Nicholas von Zinzendorf and the Moravian Brethren. Identify fruits of revival in their lives. How were they different after their encounters with the grace of Christ?

2 Suppose you were standing in front of Jesus as He suffered and died on the cross. He says, "All this I did for you. What have you done for me?" How would your love and service reflect your gratitude for His grace?
- ❏ a. I've chosen to love and serve the Lord faithfully because of His grace.
- ❏ b. I'm afraid my love and service would show little gratitude for His grace.

3 Now that you've studied Jesus' work on the cross for you and the benefits of His grace, what difference will that make in your service to Him? Check your response or write your own.
- ❏ a. My love has deepened. I want to obey His invitations to service.
- ❏ b. I've been reminded of His love, and I want to continue to be faithful in my service to Him.
- ❏ c. I'm not willing to pay the price to demonstrate my gratitude to Him.
- ❏ d. Other: _____

4 The Moravians were so in love with Jesus that they prayed, they gave, and they went all over the world seeking to "win for the Lamb that was slain the rewards of His suffering." What will you do to tell this good news about Jesus to those who need to hear?

_____

_____

_____

5 Have you ever experienced this kind of love for Christ, the wounded Savior, as you have celebrated Communion or the Lord's Supper?
    ❏ Yes   ❏ No

Pray that God will intensify your love for Christ. Ask Him to help you and your church love Him so deeply that your lives and your church will have a dramatic impact for the cause of Christ around the world. ↑

Nicholas von Zinzendorf and the Moravian Revival

Nicholas von Zinzendorf, a nobleman by birth, had been single-focused since childhood. His life motto was "I have one passion: it is Jesus, Jesus only."[1]

Yet in spite of his long-time commitment to Christ, he was unprepared to be so moved by God's Spirit while visiting an art gallery in Duesseldorf. His attention was captured by a painting of the suffering Christ, "Ecce Homo," under which were the words "This have I done for thee; what doest thou for Me?"[2] Stirred by this challenge, Zinzendorf returned to his estate. For several years he had provided shelter to a few hundred religious refugees from Moravia; to these brothers and sisters he brought home this stirring message from the suffering Savior.

On August 13, 1727, this group celebrated the Lord's Supper. As they focused their worship on the wounded Savior, their hearts were filled with love for Him who had died for them, and they sensed an awesome presence of the living Christ. That event forever changed Zinzendorf and the rest of that assembly. Look at the difference the Savior made in their lives from that day forward:

- On August 24, 48 men and women began the practice that 2 persons each hour around the clock would pray for Christ's kingdom work around the world. This began what became known as the Hundred-Year Prayer Meeting as others took up the task of praying for missions.
- More than 100 of those present at that initial Lord's Supper eventually went around the world to "win for the Lamb that was slain the rewards of His suffering." Most worked to earn a living so that they could preach the gospel free of charge.
- The first 2 missionaries sent out from the group went to Saint Thomas. They had been told that the slave owners would not permit them to preach to the slaves, so they left Germany intent on selling themselves into slavery to be able to share the gospel freely. On arriving in Saint Thomas, they found an open door and were able to work as carpenters and preach the gospel for free.
- Another group of Moravians met John Wesley on a boat headed for America. He was so moved by their living faith that he began to evaluate his own faith. Later at a Moravian chapel at Aldersgate, John Wesley was converted. He went to Germany to meet Zinzendorf and these Moravians. Wesley went on from there to lead the Evangelical Revival in England and the First Great Awakening in America. ✝

---

1. John Greenfield, *Power from on High: The Story of the Great Moravian Revival of 1727* (Bethlehem, PA: The Moravian Church in America, 1928), 20.
2. Ibid.

downpour

Spirit in control: a picture of power

PART 1

Spirit in control: a picture of power

PART 1

key verse to memorize

"Do not get drunk with wine, for that is debauchery, but be filled with the Spirit."

Ephesians 5:18

For session 10 plans, turn to page 173 in the leader guide.

discussion guide on week 9: Christ on the cross, part 2

1. What have you learned about God's "sea of grace" (p. 122, Mic. 7:18-19)?
2. Review your answers to activity 2 on page 129 and discuss what grace does and the results it produces.
3. Volunteers, share your response to activity 1 on page 125 and a brief example of how you've experienced freedom from the power of sin.
4. What prejudices have you experienced or observed from Christians (see activity 2, p. 126)?
5. How thoroughly have you been delivered from the failures of your past (see activity 1, p 128)?
6. Volunteers, describe your experience of explaining grace to someone (day 4).
7. Share your responses to the activities on page 131.
8. In smaller groups of three persons of the same gender, ask one person at a time, *How may we pray for you to experience the full benefits of grace* (freedom from the penalty and power of sin, from prejudice and from your past)? Then pray for that person. Continue for each person in the group.

dvd session 10 message notes (30 minutes)

Scripture focus: Ephesians 5:18

1. Learning about the Holy Spirit's _____
   A. The Holy Spirit is _____.
   - The names of God (1 Cor. 6:11; Acts 16:7; Rom. 8:15).
   - The attributes of God (1 Cor. 2:11; Ps. 139:7-10; Job 33:4).
   B. The Holy Spirit is _____ (Gen. 1:2; Luke 1:35).
   - Pictures in Scripture—dove, fire and wind, oil, water (Matt. 3:16; Acts 2:1-3; 10:38; John 7:38-39)

snapshot summary
The Holy Spirit is God, and He is active and personal. God wants you to be filled with the Holy Spirit and live in His power.

my goals for you
I want you to understand who the Holy Spirit is and what it means to be filled with the Holy Spirit. And I want you to demonstrate your willingness to surrender to His filling.

- The Holy Spirit is doing a whole lot in this world (John 5:6; 2 Pet. 1:21; John 14:16; 16:8; 1 Thess. 2:13).

C. The Holy Spirit is _____.

- Mind (1 Cor. 2:11); emotions (Eph. 4:30); will (1 Cor. 12:11)
- *Revival:* more of the Holy Spirit in me

2. Living in the Holy Spirit's _____

- You must be filled with the Spirit (Eph. 5:18). *Filled:* controlled, intoxicated, permeated, thoroughly influenced, overcome by a power greater than your own.
- It's a command. It's possible. It's passive. It's plural. It's repeated.
- Baptized into one body (1 Cor. 12:13). One baptism, many fillings
- Sealed with the Holy Spirit (Eph. 1:13)
- Illustrated by drunkenness (Eph. 5:18; Luke 1:15; Acts 2:4,13-15)

Testimony: James and Kathy had to trust the Lord with their kids, finances, and church. "Take every thought captive" (2 Cor. 10:3-5).

Message-notes blanks: presence, God, active, personal, power

responding to the message
1. Review by answering the following questions.
   a. What evidence from Scripture indicates that the Holy Spirit is God?
   b. How do you know the Holy Spirit is personal?
   c. What does being filled with the Holy Spirit mean?
2. Read the Scriptures listed (under 1B.) for scriptural pictures of the Holy Spirit and identify the pictures described (like dove).
3. Read the Scriptures listed above indicating the "Holy Spirit is doing a whole lot in this world" (under 1B.). What is He doing?

4. Volunteers, can you testify to ways you have experienced spiritual warfare like James and Kathy as you have sought a downpour of God's Spirit in recent weeks and months? How?

preview statements for this week's study

- Every good thing God wants to shower on your life comes through the instrumentality of the Holy Spirit.
- The power to live the Christian life is "Christ in you, the hope of glory" (Col. 1:27).
- I've never seen the Holy Spirit, but I've seen His powerful wind blowing through people's lives. Is He blowing in yours?
- Everything we've talked about in relationship to the revival God wants to bring to your life comes through the Spirit of God.
- God doesn't command things that aren't possible. Every person who has turned from sin and has embraced Christ by faith can be filled with the Spirit.
- The real issue is, Does the Holy Spirit have all of you?
- One baptism, many fillings

day 1 | Christ in You—The Holy Spirit

Every good thing God wants to shower on your life comes through the instrumentality of the Holy Spirit. Everything. The fruit of the Spirit, understanding of God's Word, love of worship, strength in a trial, grace to forgive, compassion for the lost, comfort in heartache, boldness in witnessing, power in ministry—all of this is yours when you live the Christian life in the Spirit's power. And conversely, none of it is yours when you attempt to live the Christian life any other way. Besides the Holy Spirit, God has made no other provision for you to live the Christian life.

❶ For which of the following do you sense a need for a fresh work of the Holy Spirit in your life? Check all that apply.
- ❏ Fruit of the Spirit
- ❏ Understanding God's Word
- ❏ Love of worship
- ❏ Strength in trial
- ❏ Grace to forgive
- ❏ Compassion for the lost
- ❏ Comfort in heartache
- ❏ Boldness in witness
- ❏ Power in ministry

The Holy Spirit is the power. Galatians 2:20 says, "I have been crucified with Christ. It is no longer I who live, but Christ who lives in me." There is no Christian life apart from Christ in you, and Christ is only in you *by His Holy Spirit.* Jesus told His disciples that if He went away, the Comforter would come. In John 14:16-17 Jesus said the Holy Spirit would be in them forever. "He will be in you." That's the promise of the Holy Spirit—not Jesus by your side talking to you but His Holy Spirit *in* you actually living the Christian life through you.

❷ Where does the Holy Spirit live? Check one.
- ❑ a. Only in heaven
- ❑ b. Only in my preacher
- ❑ c. In me, praise the Lord!

Yes, He's not far off and inaccessible. The Holy Spirit of Christ has been placed in you if you've come to Christ by faith for salvation. With our will we can obediently respond to what we know pleases God—like worshiping, walking with, and working for Christ. But the power to live the Christian life is "Christ in you, the hope of glory" (Col. 1:27). That's why Jesus said to the disciples, "Stay in the city until you are clothed with power from on high" (Luke 24:49). The disciples probably wanted to formulate a plan for building the church. "Can't we work on the brochures?" But Jesus told them to wait for the Holy Spirit. He knew they didn't have the capacity to do anything in their own power. "You will receive power when the Holy Spirit has come upon you, and you will be my witnesses" (Acts 1:8). "When you have the Holy Spirit," He was saying, "you'll be able to do it all."

❸ What is the one secret of effectively living the Christian life? Check one.
- ❑ a. A strong work ethic
- ❑ b. A good Christian education
- ❑ c. A godly pastor who preaches the Word
- ❑ d. The indwelling Holy Spirit, who guides and empowers

All of these things are valuable to the Christian life, but without the Holy Spirit none of the other things are sufficient for effectively living the Christian life. The effective Christian life is yieldedness to the Spirit of Christ living His life in you. In these final two weeks I want to remind you what the Bible says about the Holy Spirit; how you can experience His ongoing, indwelling, over-coming presence in your life today; and what to do when you don't.

The Spirit Is God

Every bit as much as the Father and the Son, the Holy Spirit eternally exists as a distinct and separate person yet one with the Trinity. Now I don't under-stand the doctrine of the Trinity; all human illustrations fall short. I remember having the Trinity explained to me as water. It can be liquid, it can be solid like ice, and it can be vapor. No, no, that's not really it. Well, it's like an egg, others explained. It's like the shell and the white and the yolk—no, no, it's a mystery. I think it's good to accept that there are mysteries in the Bible. We get too easily arrogant, overly clever, and human-centered when we think we've got the answer to a mystery.

Deuteronomy 29:29 says, "The secret things belong to the LORD our God, but the things that are revealed belong to us." God has not fully explained how the doctrine of the Trinity fits together (as if we could grasp it even then), but He has given us glimpses into this mystery throughout His Word.

Trinity means *tri-unity.* Three in one—Father, Son, and Holy Spirit. Deuter-onomy 6:4 points us to the Father: "Hear, O Israel: The LORD our God, the LORD is one." Affirming His place in the Trinity, Jesus said in John 10:30, "I and the Father are one." At Jesus' baptism in Luke 3:22, as Jesus came out of the water, the Spirit descended in the form of a dove, and a voice from heaven said, "You are my beloved Son; with you I am well pleased," affirming all three persons of the Trinity. The same affirmation is seen in Matthew 28:19: "Go therefore and make disciples of all nations, baptizing them in the name of the Father and of the Son and of the Holy Spirit."

4 **Which two of the following are better descriptions of *Trinity?* Check two.**
- ❑ a. It's like water—liquid, solid (ice), and vapor.
- ❑ b. God the Father, Son, and Spirit are three in one.
- ❑ c. It's a mystery beyond our understanding or explanation.
- ❑ d. It's like an egg—shell, white, and yolk.

(Answers: b, c)

The Spirit Has the Attributes of God

You may ask, James, why are you so insistent that the Spirit is God? Because Scripture is. Repeatedly, Scripture refers to different attributes of the Spirit as verifying His Deity. The Holy Spirit is called by the names of God. In 1 Corinthians 6:11 He is called the "Spirit of our God." In Acts 16:7 He is called the "Spirit of Jesus." In Romans 8:15 He is called the "Spirit of adoption," which means He participates in applying salvation.

Because we were created in God's image, man mimics some of God's characteristics, but three character traits describe *only* God.

The Holy Spirit is omniscient. He knows everything. First Corinthians 2:11 says, "Who knows a person's thoughts except the spirit of that person, which is in him? So also no one comprehends the thoughts of God except the Spirit of God." Whatever you know about God was taught to you by the Spirit of God, who is in you. We can't figure out anything about God on our own.

The Holy Spirit is omnipresent. Psalm 139:7-8 says, "Where shall I go from your Spirit? Or where shall I flee from your presence? If I ascend to heaven, you are there! If I make my bed in Sheol, you are there!" Can you run away from God? If we could bring Jonah in to testify, he'd set us straight: you can't outrun God; He's everywhere.

The Holy Spirit is omnipotent. Job admits, "The Spirit of God has made me, and the breath of the Almighty gives me life" (Job 33:4). So the Spirit of God had a specific role in creation itself. He's all-powerful.

5 **What are four reasons we know the Holy Spirit is God? I've listed one for you. Fill in the blanks for the other three.**
- ❑ 1. In Scripture the Holy Spirit is called by the names of God.
- ❑ 2. The Holy Spirit is omni _____ .
- ❑ 3. The Holy Spirit is omni _____ .
- ❑ 4. The Holy Spirit is omni _____ .

❧ **Take time to confess to the Lord the truths you've studied about Him today. Thank God for placing in you the Spirit of His Son. Praise Him for His all-knowledge, all-presence, and all-power. Give the Holy Spirit permission to guide your life into powerful effectiveness for the Lord. Ask Him what He would have you do.** ✝

| # The Holy Spirit Is Like ...

When we encounter something beyond our ability to describe, we often try to compare it to something we know. In Scripture God makes Himself known in familiar pictures. For example, God says through the psalmist He's a mountain (see Ps. 125:2), a king (see Ps. 95:3), and a shield (see Ps. 18:2). All of these are pictures of the Father. Jesus made Himself known in pictures too. He said He's a vine (see John 15:1), a door (see John 10:9), and the bread of life (see John 6:48). Scripture also gives pictures of the Holy Spirit. Here are five ways He makes Himself known to us.

❶ As you read the following paragraphs, circle the five pictures of the Holy Spirt. What is He like? How has He revealed Himself?

Dove. Matthew 3:16 tells us, "When Jesus was baptized, immediately he went up from the water, and behold, the heavens were opened to him, and he saw the Spirit of God descending like a dove and coming to rest on him." The concept that the Spirit is like a dove appears in all four Gospels. So popular is this picture that the dove has become the universal symbol of the Holy Spirit. According to Leviticus 12:6, the dove was one of the few sacrifices acceptable to God in the Old Testament because of its purity.

Fire and wind. Acts 2:1-3 relates, "When the day of Pentecost arrived, they were all together in one place. And suddenly there came from heaven a sound like a mighty rushing wind, and it filled the entire house where they were sitting. And divided tongues as of fire appeared to them." There's some debate about exactly what they saw, but the Holy Spirit is definitely described here as fire and wind.

This isn't the first time the Spirit was compared to fire. Isaiah 4:4 says the Holy Spirit is a "spirit of burning." Exodus 24:17 says, "The appearance of the glory of the LORD was like a devouring fire." John the Baptist promised that when Jesus came, He would baptize with the Holy Spirit and fire (see Luke 3:16). Again, the Holy Spirit is pictured as a purifier.

❷ Use the words *purifier* and *purity* to describe the two symbols below.
1. As a dove the Holy Spirit represents _____ .
2. As fire the Holy Spirit represents His function as _____ .

I love the picture of the Holy Spirit as wind. We have a lot of wind in Chicago. It blows the trees all the time. The distinctive thing about wind is that you never see it. You see only its effects. It's the same with the Spirit. We never see Him; we see only what He does. Jesus, talking to Nicodemus, said in John 3:8, "The wind blows where it wishes, and you hear its sound, but you do not know where it comes from or where it goes. So it is with everyone who is born of the Spirit." I've seen the Holy Spirit's effect in many people, especially in our church. I've seen God changing them and challenging them, stretching them and growing them. I've never seen the Holy Spirit, but I've seen His powerful wind blowing through people's lives. Is He blowing in yours?

Oil. In Scripture the pouring of oil is a picture of the Holy Spirit when someone was anointed. Oil represented God's blessing and favor. When Aaron became a priest in Exodus 29:7 the people were instructed to take oil, pour it on his head, and anoint him. When Samuel chose first Saul and then David to be the king, the first thing he did was to anoint them with oil (see 1 Sam. 9:16; 16:13). Acts 10:38 recalls that "God anointed Jesus of Nazareth with the Holy Spirit and with power." Anointing with oil beautifully pictures God's favor washing over someone. It is an extravagant blessing as oil covers the head. Oil therefore pictures the fullness of the Holy Spirit in our lives.

Water. As we've studied in this course, water is also a picture of the Holy Spirit. Jesus Himself framed this meaningful metaphor in John 7:37-39: "On the last day of the feast, the great day, Jesus stood up and cried out, 'If anyone thirsts, let him come to me and drink. Whoever believes in me, as the Scripture has said, "Out of his heart will flow rivers of living water."' Now this he said about the Spirit, whom those who believed in him were to receive."

To fully identify with this picture, you have to put yourself in the temple in Jesus' day at the time of that feast, the Jewish thanksgiving holiday named Sukkot (Festival of Tabernacles), which took place at the end of the dry season. As we learned in chapter 1, Israel had two seasons—wet and dry. If they didn't get rain in the spring and fall, they didn't eat the next year. So a big part of Sukkot was asking God for rain again next year. At the climax of this week of thanksgiving, the last day of the feast, the crowds poured into the temple in Jerusalem for the water ceremony, where they chanted prayers for God to bring rain for the next year.

This crowded scene was the context for Jesus' bold invitation. Just imagine: as the people cried for rain, Jesus shouted His offer: "Are you thirsty? Come to Me!" He must have made a stunning impact! John 7:39 explains that when He promised that rivers of water would flow from their hearts, He was promising the Holy Spirit. Jesus was promising life and revival to anyone who believed in Him.

③ See if you can match the symbol of the Holy Spirit on the left with its meaning for us on the right. Write a letter beside the number.

___ 1. dove	a. Evidence of His invisible work
___ 2. fire	b. Refreshing downpour for life and vitality
___ 3. wind	c. Purity
___ 4. oil	d. Blessing and favor
___ 5. water	e. Purifying

(Answers: 1–c, 2–e, 3–a, 4–d, 5–b)

Pray and ask the Holy Spirit to manifest Himself in your life in these ways. Has He been purifying your life and producing purity? Thank Him. Are you beginning to sense His blessing and favor? Continue walking in obedience. Can you testify to the evidence of the Spirit blowing through your life? Tell somebody the good things He has done. ↑

The Holy Spirit Is Active and Personal

You can be sure of this: the Holy Spirit isn't sitting around playing cards. He's active at this very moment. When we talk about all the Lord is doing in our lives, in the church, and throughout the world, we're talking about the work of the Holy Spirit. We try not to overemphasize this person of the Trinity because Scripture tells us that the Holy Spirit's heart and mission is to make Jesus known (see John 15:26). The Holy Spirit doesn't want to be in the spotlight. He wants the spotlight to be focused on the Son, Jesus Christ.

The Holy Spirit was active in the incarnation of Christ from the very beginning. When the angel told Mary she was going to give birth to Jesus, she asked, "How's this going to happen? How am I going to give birth to God's Son?" Luke 1:35 reports how the angel answered her: "The Holy Spirit will come upon you, and the power of the Most High will overshadow you; therefore the child to be born will be called holy—the Son of God." The mysterious, miraculous conception of the God-Man Jesus Christ was a ministry of the Holy Spirit.

The Spirit Is a Person

We must never accept the heresy that the Holy Spirit is just a force or an influence. The Arians taught in the early church that the Holy Spirit was the exerted energy of God, the result of God's work but not a person. The Socians at the time of the Reformation taught the same thing. Later, theologians like Friedrich Schleiermacher, the Unitarians, and most neoorthodox theologians denied the distinct personality of the Holy Spirit. Today Mormons and Jehovah's Witnesses do not believe that the Holy Spirit is God but the force or the influence of God.

If somebody from one of these cults ends up on your front porch, can you prove the Spirit's personhood from Scripture? Let's think it through for a moment. If the Holy Spirit is really a person, He should have the attributes of personhood. As evidence of a soul, you need to have a mind, emotions, and a will. Does the Holy Spirit have these elements of personhood? *Yes, He does.*

Corinthians 2:11 says the Holy Spirit has *intellect*, the capacity to know. Ephesians 4:30 says we can grieve the Holy Spirit; therefore, He has *emotions*. First Corinthians 12:11 says the Holy Spirit chooses which gift to give to believers "as he *wills*" (emphasis added).

The Holy Spirit has a mind, emotions, and a will. The Holy Spirit is not just the *force* of God; He's not just *influenced* by God; He *is* God. The Holy Spirit is moving right now, using God's Word to illuminate truth in our lives, convicting us of sin, calling us to righteousness, and reminding us of the reality of judgment.

Everything related to the revival God wants to bring to your life comes through the Spirit of God. If you don't have the Holy Spirit's power, you'll never know real, growing, genuine faith in God. At the end of the day, revival is more of the Holy Spirit actively working, stirring, and moving in you.

Ready to move now from doctrine to practice? We now have a foundation from which to build our relationship with God—the Spirit. In addition to knowing this truth, we need to experience His personal ministry in our lives. I want so much for you to be transformed by His power. Without that power you will never realize the change you have been striving for. Start today by spending some personal time with Him.

> **The Holy Spirit is the active person of Jesus Christ living in You. He has a mind, emotions, and a will. He wants to do special things in your life. I want you to take some time—more than just a brief moment—to spend alone with Him. Talk to Him. Praise Him. Thank Him for the work He has already done and is doing in your life. Invite Him to continue revealing what needs to change in your life for you to experience His fullness. Enjoy His sweet presence. ✝**

day 4 | Living in the Holy Spirit's Power

One of the most important verses in all of Scripture about the Holy Spirit is Ephesians 5:18. That is the key Scripture I've encouraged you to memorize this week. If you haven't been memorizing the recommended Scriptures in this study, I encourage you to start hiding God's Word in your mind and heart.

❶ Fill in the blanks to complete this week's memory verse.

"Do not get _____ with _____,

for that is debauchery,

but be _____ with the _____" (Eph. _____).

Because I'm a pastor, people frequently ask me questions about how to fix their lives. "I'm having a hard time loving my husband the way I should," someone says. "What should I do?" Answer: You need to be filled with the Spirit.

"You talk all the time about the responsibilities and joys of serving Christ," someone tells me. "I know I should work in the church, but I really don't have the time. What do I need?" Answer: You need to be filled with the Spirit.

Another declares, "I like my stuff more than I like my church. Don't talk anymore about giving to God because I have no intention of giving up money that could buy me more stuff. What do I need?" Answer: You need to be filled with the Spirit. Whatever the spiritual deficiency or challenge, the answer is …

❷ You know it by now. What's the answer?

Be _____

If you don't want what God wants for your life, you're not being filled with the Spirit. The Holy Spirit changes your priorities and your goals when He fills your life. Let's define what we mean by that Spirit filling. The Greek word used here means *to be filled, controlled, intoxicated, thoroughly influenced*. Here's a free Bible-study tip: if you want to understand a word in Scripture, look at ways it's used in other places in Scripture.

In Luke 4:28 religious leaders listening to Jesus were "filled" with rage. In Acts 13:45 certain Jews were "filled" with jealousy at Paul and Barnabas' success. Being filled means to be overcome by a power greater than your own.

I learned what it feels like to be filled with pain when I caught my big toe on the end of a piece of furniture and ripped the top half of my nail off. When you're filled with something, that's all there is. In this case: PAIN!

I know what it's like to be filled with joy. I remember our wedding day. Seeing Kathy coming down the aisle, I was filled with joy. There was nothing else—just that. I remember when each of our three children came into the world, and I held them for the first time. There was nothing but joy. Being filled is being completely, totally, thoroughly captured.

③ "Be filled with the Spirit" (Eph. 5:18) is packed with meaning. As you read the following paragraphs, underline the four truths.

1. "Be filled" is a command. God doesn't ever say, "Why don't you give some thought to this?" Thankfully, God doesn't command things that aren't possible. Every person who has turned from sin and has embraced Christ by faith can be filled with the Spirit. Because God commands it, it is possible.

The work of God's Spirit is not limited to filling, but it is the only ministry of the Spirit in which you participate. Here's a fly-by of the Spirit's ministry to us at conversion: you looked to Jesus Christ by faith; the Spirit convicted you of sin; you turned from that sin, found the Lord at the cross, and received Him for the forgiveness of sins; and the Spirit indwelled you. The Spirit then immersed you into the body of Christ (see 1 Cor. 12:13) and sealed your place with God (see Eph. 1:13) so that it can never be taken away. Nowhere in Scripture are you commanded to be indwelled by the Spirit or sealed by God's Spirit or baptized by God's Spirit. These happened by the Spirit's power. As a child of God, you were given all of the Holy Spirit at conversion. The real issue is, Does the Holy Spirit have all of you?

2. "Be filled" is passive in the original language. If you remember your English grammar, passive tense refers to something that is acted on. God is implied as the source of the filling, and we are the object acted on. You can't fill yourself. Only God fills you with His Holy Spirit; what you can do is ask Him to do so.

3. "Be filled" in the original language is plural. Spirit filling is not for the spiritually elite. It's not just for your pastor, your small group leader, or someone else you think has a direct connection with God. Spirit filling is for all believers.

4. "Be filled" is repeated. The verb in the original tense is continuous action. Some translations write, "Be being filled." Believers at Pentecost were filled once in Acts 2:4, and the same believers were filled again in Acts 4:8. Paul was filled with the Holy Spirit in Acts 9:17 and again in Acts 13:9. In contrast, we were baptized once into the body of Christ at conversion. That's when He came to indwell us. One baptism, many fillings.

❹ Mark each statement *T* for *true* or *F* for *false*.

___ 1. "Be filled" is possible only for the spiritually elite.

___ 2. You were given all of the Holy Spirit at conversion.

___ 3. Only God can fill you. You can't do it yourself.

___ 4. "Be filled" is one of many suggestions in Scripture. Pick the ones you like.

___ 5. There are many baptisms and only one filling.

(Answers: T–2, 3; F–1, 4, 5)

❺ The last statement is false. Write it correctly below.

_____ baptism, _____ fillings.

Now think about this. It's just a regular thing to be thirsty every day, isn't it? Drink a big glass of water, let a few hours go by, and you're thirsty again. That's the way it is with the Holy Spirit. You're filled with His power, you're living in a way that brings you and God great satisfaction and joy, but before long you're thirsty again—you need a refill of God's power from His indwelling Spirit every day. Sanctification is giving God total control of yourself—day after day being filled again.

At some time we have all taken a backward step in our spiritual lives. When we do, we forfeit the filling of the Holy Spirit. When I say or do something that deeply saddens the Holy Spirit, I forfeit His control. Because of this, I begin every day with a prayer: "Lord, fill me with Your Holy Spirit today." Sometimes throughout the day I've got to turn back to the Lord and say, "Forgive me for that thought. Forgive me for that word. Fill me again with Your Holy Spirit. Control me now." To be really filled with the Holy Spirit, you have an almost tangible sense of the Holy Spirit controlling you.

Want to be under the influence of something? Don't choose wine and drunkenness. Be controlled by the Spirit. God's Spirit wants to control your body, your emotions, and your mind. When you're controlled by the Spirit, He influences what you do and say. The Spirit of God can be an amazing guide, controlling what you think in your mind. If you're trapped in a negative pattern of thinking—anger, resentment, bitterness, frustration, impatience, fear, or worry—the Spirit of God can direct what your mind dwells on. How desperately we need the Spirit of God to control our emotions! When the Spirit is in control, life is a whole lot better.

Describe to the Lord your willingness and desire to be filled with His Spirit. Ask Him to make clear to you anything in your life that stands in the way of His filling and controlling your life, mind, and spirit. Ask Him for His power to put away all those things. Then invite Him to fill you. Take a big drink of the water of life. Quench that thirst. ↑

day 5 | A Picture of Power in the First 120 Followers of Christ

① Read about the picture of personal revival for the first 120 followers of Christ on page 146 and in Acts 2–4. Watch for ways these ordinary people experienced extraordinary things, supernatural things, through the presence and power of the Holy Spirit.

② What kind of church growth did they experience? See Acts 2:41,47; 4:4.

_____

_____

③ Read Acts 2:42-47 below. What practice or characteristic of this church appeals to you the most? Underline it.

> *They devoted themselves to the apostles' teaching and fellow-ship, to the breaking of bread and the prayers. And awe came upon every soul, and many wonders and signs were being done through the apostles. And all who believed were together and had all things in common. And they were selling their posses-sions and belongings and distributing the proceeds to all, as any had need. And day by day, attending the temple together and breaking bread in their homes, they received their food with glad and generous hearts, praising God and having favor with all the people. And the Lord added to their number day by day those who were being saved.*
>
> **Acts 2:42-47**

④ Circle words or phrases in the previous passage that describe things you wish were true of Christ's church today.

⟩ Pray and ask the Lord to cleanse and empower the Christians in your church in such a way that you will experience His life and power and productivity. ✝

The First 120 Followers of Christ: A Picture of God's Power

ACTS 2–4

If Christianity had been left up to the disciples, it would have dried up and died shortly after they watched Jesus ascend into the clouds. It would have lasted a couple of weeks at best, and then their lack of power would have ended in disillusionment. Spiritual fervor would have been a distant memory of something special but short-lived. *Why can't we make this work?* would haunt their thinking.

But history testifies that is not what happened. The 11 disciples, along with Jesus' earthly mother and brothers, formed the core of 120 people who could not and would not deny that something supernatural had occurred in the life, death, resurrection, and ascension of Jesus. Furthermore, something supernatural had occurred in them when they believed He was who He claimed to be—Messiah, Savior, Lord, God! Somehow they sensed that they were living at the hinge point of history. But once Jesus had left the earth, they didn't know what to do other than what He had told them to do—wait (see Acts 1:4).

A few days earlier Jesus' promise had sounded like a riddle: "It is to your advantage that I go away, for if I do not go away, the Helper will not come to you. But if I go, I will send him to you. And when he comes, he will convict the world concerning sin and righteousness and judgment" (John 16:7-8).

But with that promise came the secret to this new life: "You will receive *power* when the Holy Spirit has come upon you, and you will be my witnesses" (Acts 1:8, emphasis added). These 120 people had repented of their sin and had confessed Him as their Savior and Lord. Now God gave them the supernatural thing they needed to bear His name—He gave them power. New strength was breathed into them. Individuals doing business with God were individually connected to the power of the universe.

Did anyone notice? These Spirit-filled people were the talk of the town! What happened to them? One day they are hiding and running and denying they even know Christ, and the next they are standing on the street corner shouting the good news. Where did this boldness, eloquence, and authority come from? The same source it comes from today. Every day we're presented with a new opportunity for Him to fill us with His life so that we can experience God's power in a way we never could apart from Him.

What was the result? When these uneducated, unsophisticated, insecure followers of Jesus were filled with the power of God's Spirit, Acts 17:6 says they "turned the world upside down." The world is still turning on the power of God at work in every Spirit-filled follower of Christ. ✝

week 11

Spirit in control:
a picture of power

PART 2

Spirit in control: a picture of power

PART 2

a verse to memorize

"If you live according to the flesh you will die, but if by the Spirit you put to death the deeds of the body, you will live."

Romans 8:13

For session 11 plans, turn to page 174 in the leader guide.

discussion guide on week 10: Spirit in control, part 1

1. What are some good things God showers on us through the Holy Spirit (see activity 1, p. 136)? Volunteers, share a testimony about a time you experienced one of these works of the Spirit.
2. Suppose a cult member came to your door and claimed that the Holy Spirit is not God. What truths would you use to explain that He is God? Find a Scripture for each truth in day 1.
3. Name five things the Holy Spirit is like. What benefit for us does each symbolize (see activity 3, p. 140)?
4. Suppose a Christian came to your group and stated that his life needs to be fixed. Explain what he needs to do. What truths can you share with him from Ephesians 5:18 about being filled with the Spirit (see day 4)?
5. Share and discuss your responses to activities 2–4 on page 145. Pray that God will so fill your church with His Spirit that members will experience His presence and power in fellowship with one another.

dvd session 11 message notes (29 minutes)

Scripture focus: Romans 8:9-17

Am I filled with the Holy Spirit _____?

• Anyone who belongs to Him has the Spirit of Christ (Rom. 8:9).

• By the Spirit you put to death the deeds of the body (Rom. 8:13).

Proofs of the Holy Spirit's filling:

1. _____ (Rom. 8:14)
2. _____ (Rom. 8:15)
3. _____ (Rom. 8:15)
4. _____ (Rom. 8:16)

snapshot summary

You can be filled and empowered by the Holy Spirit of God in ways that show in your life. You can know you are filled.

my goals for you

I want you to understand how you can be filled with the Holy Spirit and how to avoid grieving and quenching Him. And I want you to demonstrate your surrender to Him so that you can be filled.

How to lose the filling of the Holy Spirit:
- We grieve the Spirit (Eph. 4:30).
- We quench the Spirit (1 Thess. 5:19).

5. _____ (Rom. 8:17)

How to be filled with the Holy Spirit:
- _____ all known sin to God (1 John 1:9).
- _____ God to fill you (Luke 11:11-13).
- _____ that He has filled you (Mark 11:24).

Message music: see the "Come, Let Us Return" lyrics on page 150.

responding to the message

1. Review by answering the following questions.
   a. What are five proofs that the Holy Spirit is filling you now? Volunteers, share times when you experienced one of these proofs as the Holy Spirit has revealed Himself in you.
   b. How can we lose the filling of the Holy Spirit? Give examples.
   c. What are three steps you can take to be filled with the Holy Spirit?
2. Look at the front cover of your *Downpour* book. Describe the spiritual symbolism you see in the image of the man standing in the rain. Take time for sentence prayers that God will send His refreshing rain. Thank Him for all you've already experienced of His downpour. Be specific.
3. One more time form small, same-gender groups of three. Ask one person at a time, *How may we pray for you?* Then pray.

Message-notes blanks: now, leading me, gives confidence, intimacy, security, identity, Confess, Ask, Believe

See the preview statements for this week on page 151.

Come, Let Us Return

awesome God, lifted high, / seated on the throne
ruling glorious, robed in splendor, / universe Your own
Holy, Holy, Holy sing the seraph as they fly
purging coal of sovereign grace, / calling forth this cry

come, let us return, let us return unto our King!
He has torn, but He will heal us,
bring Him everything
self and sin and shame we're spurning,
grief and sorrow now are burning,
yes it's time we are returning, to the Lord

mirror of Your holiness, / showing me my sin
grief and shame displacing all the / darkness that's within
changing mind and heart reveal / i've no one else to blame
falling in repentance, / from our brokenness proclaim...

Christ upon the cross of shame, / we see who put You there
merciful, atoning Savior / dies for our despair
so unworthy of the blood / that covers all our shame
rising in the grace unearned / we're shouting the refrain...

Spirit of revival power / birthing in my soul
passionate pursuit of Jesus is my only goal
fills us with abiding joy / and conquers all our foes
bearing fruit for Jesus only, / 'til the whole world knows

———

 Read Hosea 6:1-4 and Isaiah 6:1-6 on page 151. Then slowly read the lyrics above and meditate on their meaning. Use the following questions to review the five major messages of *Downpour*.

1. God on the throne: What are some characteristics of God described in verse 1?
2. What is the wonderful promise in the chorus (second paragraph) that God does for us after He has torn us?
3. Sin in the mirror/self in the dirt: What are the negative words describing some of the consequences of sin in verse 2?
4. Christ on the cross: What has Christ done for us through His death on the cross? (verse 3)
5. What are some of the purposes of being filled with the Spirit in verse 4?

Come, let us return to the LORD; *for he has torn us, that he may heal us; he has struck us down, and he will bind us up. After two days he will revive us; on the third day he will raise us up, that we may live before him. Let us know; let us press on to know the* LORD; *his going out is sure as the dawn; he will come to us as the showers, as the spring rains that water the earth.*

Hosea 6:1-4

In the year that King Uzziah died I saw the Lord sitting upon a throne, high and lifted up; and the train of his robe filled the temple. Above him stood the seraphim. Each had six wings: with two he covered his face, and with two he covered his feet, and with two he flew. And one called to another and said: Holy, holy, holy is the Lord of hosts; the whole earth is full of his glory! And the foundations of the thresholds shook at the voice of him who called, and the house was filled with smoke. And I said: Woe is me! For I am lost; for I am a man of unclean lips, and I dwell in the midst of a people of unclean lips; for my eyes have seen the King, the Lord of hosts! Then one of the seraphim flew to me, having in his hand a burning coal that he had taken with tongs from the altar.

Isaiah 6:1-6

This week listen to the song on your Message-Music CD (track 5) at the back of this book and use the verses to review the message of *Downpour*.

Pray that the Lord will complete His refreshing and cleansing work in your life. Ask the Lord to fill you with His Holy Spirit so that you can bear fruit for Christ in faithful and powerful witness to Him.

preview statements for this week's study
- Get beyond superficial confession and take the sin that grieves God's Spirit to a place of true repentance.
- God gives the Holy Spirit to those who ask.
- God has provided no other way for you to successfully live the Christian life apart from His Spirit's filling you every moment of every day. The good news is that He promises unlimited refills.
- I'm a blood-bought child of Almighty God and an heir with Christ.
- Ignoring or resisting the Lord leads you back to that barren wasteland. By listening to God's Spirit and choosing not to grieve or quench Him, you allow His reviving work to continue unhindered.
- When we are filled with the Spirit, we talk about things that fire up our faith.

| # How to Be Filled with the Spirit

Last week we focused on the Holy Spirit and the power He provides to live the Christian life. We learned that we are to be filled with the Spirit.

❶ As a follower of Jesus, do you recognize your need to be filled with the Holy Spirit? ❑ Yes ❑ No

If your answer is yes, the following three steps will help you be filled with the Holy Spirit.

1. Repent of All Known Sin

Do what we talked about in weeks 4–5 on a regular basis. Identify the *sin in the mirror.* If you discover anything you're harboring, anything you're holding back, anything in the way, it's got to go. It grieves God's Spirit. Apply the exercises of week 7 on repentance. Get beyond superficial confession and take the sin that grieves God's Spirit to a place of true repentance.

Maybe you know the Lord, but you've lived a carnal Christian life for many years—without the filling of the Spirit because of something you won't let go of or something you won't do. You must be current with God's Spirit to be filled with God's Spirit. It's not a matter of rattling off a couple of token prayers. You can't fool God. He knows your heart.

❷ What is the first step for being filled with the Holy Spirit?

_____

❭ **Ask God, "Search me, O God, and know my heart! Try me and know my thoughts! And see if there be any grievous way in me" (Ps. 139:23).**

2. Ask God to Fill You

I love my children, and I love to give gifts to them. If we know how to give good gifts to people we love, how much more will God give the Holy Spirit to those who ask! Matthew 7:11 and Luke 11:13 reiterate this truth: if as earthly parents we "know how to give good gifts to [our] children, how much more will your Father who is in heaven give good things to those who ask Him!"

❭ **When you have dealt with all known sin through repentance, ask God to fill you with His Spirit. Open your hands and say something like this:** *Come and fill me. Lord, I want to be controlled by You. I want to know Your fullness in my life to a greater degree than ever before by Your Holy Spirit. I see my need, so please come and fill me now.*

❸ What is the second step for being filled with the Holy Spirit?

_____

downpour

3. Believe That He Has Filled You

John 14:13 affirms, "Whatever you ask in my name, this I will do, that the Father may be glorified in the Son." Matthew 9:29 promises, "According to your faith be it done to you." Refuse to doubt. Don't let your heart be filled with unbelief. Believe that God's Spirit has filled you. Express your faith to God. If you have honestly dealt with all known sin as a follower of Jesus Christ and then prayed and asked God's Spirit to fill you, He has done it!

④ What is the final step for being filled with the Holy Spirit?

_____

Continuous Revival

The Holy Spirit wants to continuously fill you, empowering you with all the intensity and life and joy that are His to give. It's like putting your hand under a stream of water rushing from a faucet. He wants to continuously fill you and satisfy you with Himself.

God's Spirit is where the power comes from to live in a place of continuous revival with Him. God has provided no other way for you to successfully live the Christian life apart from His Spirit's filling you every moment of every day. The good news is that He promises unlimited refills.

Downpour

As I write this, it's beginning to rain outside. Isn't that cool? Remember our downpour verse from Hosea 6:3:

> ## Let us know; let us press on to know the LORD; his going out is sure as the dawn; he will come to us as the showers, as the spring rains that water the earth.

What started outside my window as a drizzle has now become a downpour. Puddles on the roads are splashing up—it's an out-of-control rain! That's the way God comes to someone who seeks Him for revival. He fills us, controls us, and empowers us. He is the One who quenches our thirst. He is the One who fills up what's missing. He is the One who satisfies our deepest longings. He is the One who brings and sustains a continuous revival in our lives. That's what the Holy Spirit is doing in the lives of those who follow the path of continuous revival that we have detailed in these lessons. That's what He's doing in the lives of those of us who are pressing on to know the Lord.

Come, come, Lord Jesus; come to us like the rain. ✝

| # Proofs of the Spirit's Filling, Part 1

"How do I know whether the Holy Spirit is filling me now?" That's a good question because you *can* know; it's not subjective. In Romans 8:14-17 Paul gives us five confirmations or proofs of the Holy Spirit's filling ministry. As you read about the following proofs, ask yourself these five questions.

Proof 1: Leading Me—Is God Leading Me?

"All who are led by the Spirit of God are sons of God" (Rom. 8:14). So are you one of God's children? If you are and you're filled with the Spirit, the Spirit of God is leading you. Everyone who is born of the Spirit is led by the Spirit. He directs you in what to say, what to do, and how to do it.

By His Spirit God sovereignly directs and works in our lives, leading us by His Spirit. This is the ongoing experience of a child of God. The Lord puts you in the right place at the right time to speak for Him. He leads you to a certain person. He puts words in your mouth. This leading is evidence of being filled with the Holy Spirit.

1 **Is God leading you?** ❏ **Yes** ❏ **No**

2 **If you have experienced God leading you, briefly describe one time.**

_____

_____

_____

Proof 2: Gives Confidence—Is God Giving Me Confidence?

Romans 8:15 says, "You did not receive the spirit [attitude] of slavery to fall back into fear." Confidence is one of the overriding characteristics in the life of a person who is being filled with God's Spirit.

Fear is what you had before Christ. If you talk to people who don't know the Lord, you quickly see that they're slaves to fear—fear of the future, fear of dying, fear of not having enough. People who don't know the Lord are frequently filled with fear. But when the Spirit of God comes to live in you, He replaces that fear with confidence. We should trust the Lord. We don't know what's going to happen, but our confidence is in God. Confidence grows in the life of a person who is controlled or filled by God's Spirit.

3 **Is God giving you confidence?** ❏ **Yes** ❏ **No**

4 **If you have experienced God giving you confidence, briefly describe one time.**

_____

_____

If you see God's proofs in your life, take time to thank Him for the work of His Spirit in you. If you had to answer no to the questions today, ask the Lord to reveal the true nature of your needs. I'm pressing on to help you know His fullness. ✝

day 3 | Proofs of the Spirit's Filling, Part 2

Proof 3: Intimacy—Am I Growing in Intimacy with God?

Romans 8:15 goes on, "You have received the Spirit of adoption as sons, by whom we cry, 'Abba! Father!'" In the ancient world if a man was not happy with his heirs, he could adopt a slave as a son and give him all the rights of sonship. Romans 8:15 is saying that as children of this world who are redeemed by the precious blood of Jesus Christ, we have been adopted into God's family and have been declared and treated as sons and daughters by Almighty God. The Spirit of God has been given to us, by whom we cry out, "Abba! Father!" That's a term of intimacy. Every culture has its own phrase for this intimacy. Some kids say, "Daddy!" Others say, "Papa!" Whatever the lingo, it's tender. God's Spirit wants to bring you to a gentle place with the Lord where you call Him Abba.

Women understand intimacy with God big-time, but men are clueless. Men especially need to get to a place where we don't feel embarrassed in our private times with the Lord to call him, "Abba, Daddy! I need You. I love You. I'm hurting. I want You. I'm seeking You." You might say, "I think I would feel a little weird calling out to God like that." But the Spirit of God is trying to bring you to a place where you desire and pursue that kind of private intimacy with God.

What keeps us from doing that? Pride. "I don't want to feel anything," we say. "I'll keep God at arm's length—this far and no farther." The Spirit of God is trying to break down that pride in all of us. To be filled with His Spirit is to desire and pursue growing intimacy with God.

1 **Am I growing in intimacy with God?** ❏ **Yes** ❏ **No**

Tell God your desire to grow in intimacy with Him. Ask Him to heal and remove anything in your life that would cause you to keep Him at a distance. Ask Abba, Father, to draw you near.

Proof 4: Security—Do I Feel Secure in Christ?

Romans 8:16 says, "The Spirit himself bears witness with our spirit that we are children of God." Over and over I hear from Christians express doubt about their salvation. They ask, "Am I really a Christian? Am I really saved?" Well, news flash! One ministry of the Spirit of God is confirming to you the reality of your relationship in God's family. He wants you to know that you are really His. God's Spirit speaks security in your heart to confirm to you the reality of your place in God's family.

You may be asking, "Why don't I get all this?" You may be wondering why some of these ministries of the Holy Spirit are not a part of your spiritual experience. If you're not experiencing the confirming security of the Spirit of God in your life, if you've ever thought, *I don't know if I'm a child of God,* only repentance can restore the filling of the Holy Spirit in you. If you're not a child of God because you've never come through repentance to Christ by faith, that is the repentance you need. But there are two more reasons you may doubt: you can grieve the Holy Spirit and forfeit His filling, and you can quench the Holy Spirit and put out His fire in your heart. Tomorrow's lesson will examine these two ways you can keep the Holy Spirit silenced and power-less in your life.

2 **Do you feel secure in Christ?** ❏ **Yes** ❏ **No**

3 **If you answered no and you know it's because you've never turned to Christ in faith for the new life He offers, turn to page 18 and settle this issue now.**

Proof 5: Identify—Do I Draw My Identity from Christ?

Romans 8:17 says, "... if children, then heirs—heirs of God and fellow heirs with Christ." Do you know how rich you are? An heir has the rights to every-thing that belongs to the father. Someday all that belongs to our Heavenly Father will be yours. We live like paupers when we're children of the King because we're not experiencing the filling ministry of the Holy Spirit. To be filled with the Holy Spirit is to have Him constantly remind us of the unsearch-able riches of Christ and all that belongs to us as blood-bought children of Almighty God. That's our identity as heirs and joint-heirs with Christ. You ask, "Why don't I feel more wealthy?" That reflects the lack of the Holy Spirit's filling in your life. "I think I've lost some of that," you say. Well, start again. You don't have to earn the Holy Spirit's filling; you just have to be willing and ask. God wants to fill you with His Spirit.

4 **Which of the following best describes your identify in Christ? Check one.**
❏ a. I'm a pauper—poor, weak, and needy.
❏ b. I'm a blood-bought child of Almighty God and an heir with Christ.

5 **Are you drawing your identify from Christ?** ❏ **Yes** ❏ **No**

If you answered no to some or all of today's questions, pray that God will reveal the things in your life that are holding back the rain. If you've answered yes, take time to review the proofs and give thanks to God for every evidence of His Holy Spirit's work in your life. ☂

day 4 | Grieving & Quenching the Spirit

We're learning that only through the Holy Spirit's power can we continue to experience a downpour of spiritual blessing in our lives. The key is being filled by the Holy Spirit on a daily—even moment-by-moment—basis. In the last two days you may have asked the five questions and found that you don't have the proofs of His filling in your life. Two things can keep that from happening.

1. Grieving the Holy Spirit. Paul wrote, "Do not grieve the Holy Spirit of God, by whom you were sealed for the day of redemption" (Eph. 4:30). The word *grieve* means *to cause pain or sorrow.* Since your salvation the Holy Spirit has been and is in you—once and for all. He goes where you go; He sees what you see. He hears what you say. When you do things that do not please the Lord, it makes Him sad. Think about the sin in the mirror and the process outlined in weeks 4–5. Sin grieves the Spirit of God. Because the Spirit is sealed inside you, you make Him sad when you choose to sin. You grieve the Spirit when you do things He doesn't want you to do. So be careful not to grieve God's Spirit.

❶ Many things fall into this category of actions and words that grieve the Holy Spirit. Read Ephesians 4:29-31 below and circle words or phrases that describe ways we can grieve the Holy Spirit.

"Let no corrupting talk come out of your mouths, but only such as is good for building up, as fits the occasion, that it may give grace to those who hear. And do not grieve the Holy Spirit of God, by whom you were sealed for the day of redemption. Let all bitterness and wrath and anger and clamor and slander be put away from you, along with all malice" (Eph. 4:29-31).

Corrupt talk, bitterness, wrath, anger, clamor, slander, and malice are some of the ways we can grieve the Holy Spirit. This kind of behavior can keep you from experiencing the fullness of the Holy Spirit.

2. Quenching the Holy Spirit. First Thessalonians 5:19 makes this direct command: "Do not quench the Spirit." *Quench* means *to snuff out, douse, cool down, trim back.* To quench God's Spirit is to extinguish His intended result. That happens when we do not do the things He tells us to do. How do we put out His fire in our hearts? By ignoring and resisting His direction.

I'm sad to say that I've seen this happen in my life. The Spirit directs me to do something, and I say, "Nah." Each time He prompts me to respond and I refuse, His voice gets softer until I can't hear it anymore. That's quenching the Holy Spirit.

❷ Categorize each action by writing *G* for *grieve* and *Q* for *quench.*
___ 1. Refusing a service opportunity the Lord prompted you to accept
___ 2. Choosing to sleep instead of get up to spend time with the Lord
___ 3. Making cutting remarks that tear down a brother or a sister in Christ
___ 4. Refusing to obey a clear command in Scripture
___ 5. Saying no to the Holy Spirit's leading to witness to someone
___ 6. Causing division in the church over your preferences

(Answers: G–2, 3, 6, ; Q–1, 4, 5)

❸ Match the action on the left with the correct definition on the right.

___ 1. Grieve the Spirit   a. Doing something that makes the Holy Spirit sad

___ 2. Quench the Spirit   b. Ignoring or resisting the Holy Spirit's direction

(Answers: 1–a, 2–b)

Aggressively deal with these two areas. Ignoring or resisting the Lord leads you back to that barren wasteland. By listening to God's Spirit and choosing not to grieve or quench Him, you allow His reviving work to continue unhindered. Moments will come when you foolishly grieve and quench God's Spirit. At those times confess the sins as soon as they occur. By doing so, you welcome the filling of the Holy Spirit and avoid another long journey into carnal living and the spiritual wasteland you have worked so hard to leave behind.

❹ Activate

Reflect on these questions and respond as the Holy Spirit leads you.

- What are common ways we deeply sadden or grieve the Lord?
- Are you doing any of these now? If so, how are you grieving Him?
- What should you do now that you understand this?
- What specific issue has the Spirit been talking to you about that you have ignored?
- Have you refused to do something you know the Lord was asking of you?
- What is He saying?
- Up until now how have you resisted His Word?
- Deal with it now before you quench His voice.

Ask the Holy Spirit to set off a spiritual alarm anytime you grieve Him or quench Him.

Replicate

Our key verse for "The Spirit in Control" message has been Ephesians 5:18: "Do not get drunk with wine, for that is debauchery, but be filled with the Spirit." Verse 19 is critical for keeping the downpour of revival flowing: "… addressing one another in psalms and hymns and spiritual songs."

That's called fellowship! When we are filled with the Spirit, we talk about things that fire up our faith. You can't keep quiet when you're learning about how great God is and what He's done in your life lately. The Holy Spirit loves it when we do this.

❺ Need a conversation starter for your next time of friendly fellowship? Read Romans 8:9-17 again and review with a friend the five proofs that the Holy Spirit is filling you. Select one of these five evidences and share with someone today or tomorrow a time in your life when you clearly knew the Spirit was in control. The Holy Spirit will be listening in— and cheering you on!

1. Leading me (v. 14)—*Lately God has really impressed on me …*
2. Gives confidence (v. 15)—*God is giving me new confidence so that …*
3. Intimacy (v. 15)—*God has been drawing me closer to Himself in these areas …*

downpour

4. Security (v. 16) — *I used to struggle in my assurance of this _____, but now He's given me real security in knowing this _____.*
5. Identify (v. 17) — *You'll never believe it, but I no longer get my sense of identity from …*

Elevate

Holy Spirit of God, thank You for filling my life with You. You are in control of all that I am—my thoughts, my actions, my words, and my feelings. Thank You, Spirit of God. I am now living under the downpour of Your power and strength and blessing, and I thank You for the riches of Your mercy. In the precious name of Jesus. Amen.

day 5 | Personal Revival in Shantung

❶ Read about the picture of personal revival from the Shantung Revival in China. Pay attention to the way personal revival began to spread from one to groups to a whole school.

❷ Ask yourself the two questions of Marie Monsen. First, "Have you been born again?" ❑ Yes ❑ No

Second, "What evidence do you have of the new birth?"

_____

_____

❸ What are some steps Charles Culpepper took to get right with God and to be filled with His Spirit?

_____

_____

Pray and ask the Holy Spirit to show you any sin that still stands in the way of your being filled by Him. Ask Him to identify things you need to do to get those things right with others. Follow the steps to filling:
- Confess and repent of all known sin.
- Ask God to fill you with His Spirit.
- Believe that He has filled you.

Charles Culpepper
and the Shantung Revival

As if political unrest and evacuation weren't enough, missionaries in northern China had to face the probing questions their fellow missionary, Marie Monsen, persistently asked them: "Have you been born again?" "What evidence do you have of the new birth?"

As these relocated missionary teachers and doctors gathered for prayer and Bible study, God used these questions to prompt deep soul-searching. The humbled missionaries confessed and repented of sins and found reconciliation with God and one another. Some even realized they had never been saved, and they turned to Christ for the first time.

Missionary Charles Culpepper couldn't rest. He searched Scripture to understand what it means to be filled with the Holy Spirit. As he sincerely prayed to be filled, the Holy Spirit reminded him of past sins he had never dealt with. He wrote letters asking for forgiveness. He sent stolen money back to his college alma mater and offered to return his diploma. But still he experienced no spiritual power in his work. He felt as if his heart were stone. "What is the matter, Lord?" he asked.

Leading him to Romans 2:17-25, the Lord convicted him that he was a hypocrite and that God's name was being blasphemed among the Chinese because of him. He awoke his wife, and they prayed all night. The next day he confessed his pride to his fellow missionaries. He describes what happened next:

The Lord became more real to me than any human being had ever been. He took complete control of my soul—removing all hypocrisy, shame, and unrighteousness—and filled me with His divine love, purity, compassion, and power. During those moments, I realized my complete unworthiness and His totally sufficient mercy and grace. ...

The next day was Sunday, a new and wonderful day at our missionary church. I have never heard such praying or experienced such joyous fellowship as we had that day.

Students came back from the political displacement only to be met by teachers who had been changed by God's Spirit. They began a series of meetings that prompted great conviction of sin in the students.

For 10 days the services continued. By their end more than 1,500 students had turned to or returned to God. God had brought a downpour of blessing, first through two penetrating questions for the missionaries, whom in turn God used to impact a generation of students. [1] ↑

---

1. C. L. Culpepper, *Spiritual Awakening: The Shantung Revival* (self-published, 1982), 1–35.

downpour

He will come to us like the rain

He will come to us like the rain

key verse to memorize

"Let us know; let us press on to know the LORD;
his going out is sure as the dawn;
he will come to us as the showers,
as the spring rains that water the earth."

Hosea 6:3

For session 12 plans, turn to page 174 in the leader guide.

discussion guide on week 11: Spirit in control, part 2

1. What are three steps for being filled with the Holy Spirit (day 1, p. 152)?
2. What are five proofs of the Spirit's filling from Romans 8:14-17? Explain and give an example of each proof.
3. What does grieving the Holy Spirit mean, and how can we do it?
4. What does quenching the Holy Spirit mean, and how can we do it?
5. Volunteers, what evidence do you see in your life that the Holy Spirit is filling you? Share a response to one of the conversation starters on page 158 (activity 5). Keep your focus on what *God has done* in you.
6. Volunteers, what evidence do you have of the new birth (activity 2, p. 159)?
7. What are some of the steps Charles Culpepper took to get right with God and to be filled with His Spirit during the Shantung Revival (activity 3, p. 159)?
8. Review your responses to the message-music activity on page 150.

dvd session 12 (9 minutes)

Scripture focus: Hosea 10:12
What will this raining of righteous feel like? It may be—
• a new delight in worship;
• a new victory over sin;
• a fresh hunger for God's Word;
• all of these things and so much more.

This week's DVD is a brief musical summary of our *Downpour* study:

Message music: see the "Come, Let Us Return" lyrics on page 150.

snapshot summary

God has called us to return to Him. When we do, He comes to us in a downpour of refreshing rain of His grace and Spirit's power.

my goals for you

I want you to identify what God has done in your life over the past 11 weeks and to show your gratitude by giving testimony of His work in your life.

reviewing *Downpour*

Use some or all of the following questions or activities to review.

1. Which of the five messages listed below has been the most meaningful to you? How or why?
   - God on the Throne: A Picture of Holiness
   - Sin in the Mirror: A Picture of Brokenness
   - Self in the Dirt: A Picture of Repentance
   - Christ on the Cross: A Picture of Grace
   - Spirit in Control: A Picture of Power
2. Which memory verse has been most meaningful to you and why?
3. How has God worked in your life through the message music? Which message in song has had the greatest impact on you and why?
4. Of all the small-group experiences, learning activities, and prayer experiences you've had over the past 12 weeks, which has been the most life-changing?
5. What statements, Scriptures, ideas, or illustrations have been particularly meaningful to you?
6. Which of the following biblical and historical pictures of personal revival have been particularly meaningful, instructive, or inspirational and why?
   - Josiah (p. 15)
   - Hezekiah (p. 34)
   - David (p. 62)
   - Jonah (p. 90)
   - Peter (p. 118)
   - First 120 followers of Christ (p. 146)
   - Jonathan Edwards (p. 20)
   - Revival in Scotland (p. 48)
   - Derksen brothers (p. 76)
   - Evan Roberts (p. 104)
   - Nicholas von Zinzendorf (p. 132)
   - Charles Culpepper (p. 160)

Close your session by praying together. Lift your praise, worship, and thanksgiving to the God who sits on the throne.

Epilogue

Everything that has happened in your heart as you have read this book and have activated its truth in your heart through the application exercises has been about crisis. In the beginning I told you that downpours begin with a crisis—a crisis of returning to God. But what do we do when the crisis is over?

You may be saying, "James, I've dealt with my sin in view of God's holiness. I've repented and made restitution and reveled in the grace of the cross. I'm at a better place with God than I have been for a long time, but how do I keep it going? How do I keep the river flowing? How do I keep the downpour falling? How do I keep flourishing in my relationship with Christ? And what if I struggle, stumble, or fall?"

Those are the right questions to ask now. Let me give you a simple answer: when you *falter* in the process of continuous revival, you must *return* to the crisis. Live every moment of every day in continuous revival through the filling ministry of the Holy Spirit. Inevitably, you will stumble. When you do, go back through the weeks in this study and review these five pictures:

1. God on the Throne: A Picture of Holiness
2. Sin in the Mirror: A Picture of Brokenness
3. Self in the Dirt: A Picture of Repentance
4. Christ on the Cross: A Picture of Grace
5. Spirit in Control: A Picture of Power

These steps are a proven road to revival. If you lose your way, retrace your steps. I cannot overemphasize this point: when you fail in the process, return to the crisis. Personal revival is always available for every follower of Jesus Christ. When you realize that you've drifted away from a passionate pursuit of Christ, turn around, repent of the sin God shows you in the mirror, and take hold of the grace that is freely bestowed on all who believe.

This week I read the testimonies of 20 well-known Christian leaders in the book *They Found the Secret*. Though they led very different lives and had very diverse personalities, the spiritual lives of Hudson Taylor, Amy Carmichael, Oswald Chambers, Charles Finney, and other men and women whom God greatly used all exhibited a common pattern. All of the witnesses testified that a crisis in their Christian lives led them to experience the joy and power of a Spirit-filled life. In their lives and in yours and mine, the path that leads from a spiritually barren, dry wasteland to the abundant, overflowing life Jesus promised is the filling of the Holy Spirit.

1 **If you want to get fired up by the testimonies of men and women who found the secret of living in the victory of personal revival, get a copy of *They Found the Secret* and be blessed as you read their stories.**

As you know, revival doesn't come from trying harder or wanting it more. If it did, the church would be ablaze with fervent, obedient, fired-up worshipers. No, only one thing keeps the portals of heaven open, and it's not anything we can pump up in our flesh. Downpours come when you stand under the super-

Throw away your umbrellas and enjoy the rain

natural flow and power of God's Spirit. Christ *in you* is your hope of glory; Christ *in you* satisfies and refreshes. Being fully and gloriously controlled by His Spirit is the secret of lasting, transforming joy that produces a deeply satisfying downpour.

I praise God for the work He has done in your heart as you have applied the truths of these pages.

Close your study with a prayer of thanksgiving for all He has done.

Leader Guide

If you have not already done so, read the introduction on pages 5–6 before you continue reading this leader guide.

The following pages will help you prepare for and conduct a 12-session, small-group study of *Downpour: He Will Come to Us like the Rain*.

Understand Your Role as Leader

You do not have to be a content expert to lead this Bible study. Your role is more of a facilitator. James MacDonald will provide inspiring messages from God's Word each week in a DVD segment. During the week participants will study this workbook and complete the interactive learning activities and prayer experiences. Through these content segments and learning experiences, participants will be ready to discuss the messages and share personal insights and experiences during group sessions. The two-page spread at the beginning of each week's lessons provides a practical guide for your small-group session. On those pages you will find—

- a discussion guide for the previous week's workbook study;
- DVD message notes for the teaching segment by James MacDonald;
- suggestions to guide discussion and sharing in response to the DVD message;
- preview statements for the upcoming study content.

In many cases, following the suggestions for each of these segments, together with prayer times, will fill your small-group session. If you have more time, you may choose to use some of the additional suggestions on the pages that follow. By using these resources, you can be a lead learner along with the other group participants. You could even share leadership with another small-group member if desired or necessary.

Pray

Because this is a spiritual process in which God is involved, pray for His leadership and involvement. Pray for wisdom. Pray that God will draw participants into the study for their benefit and His renown. Pray that God will reveal Himself in His holiness and will call your members to return to Him. Pray that they will respond to the Lord in repentance. Ask God to lavish His love and grace on them and to fill them with His Spirit. Pray that God will revive not only the members of your group but your church as well.

Set a Time and a Place

The small-group sessions can take place at any time that is convenient for participants. Sundays, weekdays, or Saturdays will work, daytime or evening. We recommend 90-minute sessions so that you will have adequate time to view the DVD segments and process what God has taught and done during the week. You could try shorter sessions, but you will likely find that members do not have time to adequately process what they are learning. Plan for plenty of time for members to share and to pray together and for one another. The first group session will require 90 minutes due to the length of the DVD message.

Groups may meet at the church building, in homes or apartments, in a community meeting room, in a workplace before or after work or over lunch, in a school, or almost anyplace. The availability of a television or projector and a DVD player, sufficient space, and enough privacy to prevent interruption are the primary factors that may limit your choice of locations.

Determine Fees If Any
Each participant will need a Bible study book for the small-group study. Determine the cost for participants so that you can mention it when you advertise the course. Usually, people are more faithful to use the Bible study book and to attend group sessions when they have made a personal investment in the resource. Be prepared to provide partial or complete scholarships when needed so that no one will be excluded for financial reasons.

Establish a Closed Group
A closed group does not allow new members to join after the first or second session. Because of the sequential nature of the *Downpour* messages, members will not be able to adequately engage in the process if they have not studied all of the material. If someone wants to join the group after the first session, start a waiting list and begin a new group when you have enough members and a leader.

Set the Group Size
The best small-group dynamics take place in groups of 8 to 15 members that remain consistent over time (in this case 12 sessions). Smaller groups may be too intimate for some but are satisfactory if members know and trust one another. Larger groups are too big to allow everyone to participate. If you are really serious about helping members experience personal revival, you don't want spectators. If you have more than 15 participants, consider dividing into multiple groups. If your church has multiple groups meeting at the same time at church, you may choose to watch the DVD messages as a large group and divide into small groups for content discussion and response to the DVD message segments. If you use this format, consider keeping the people in the same small group each week. Don't require

people to get acquainted and develop new relationships each week. They need to develop trust for sharing deeper thoughts and feelings as the study progresses.

Enlist Participants
Use your church's normal channels to advertise this study: bulletins, posters, newsletters, PowerPoint® slides or video before the service, announcements, website, and so forth. The DVDs include a promotional segment (1 min., 15 sec.) that will introduce the *Downpour* message and invite participation. We assume that most participants will already have a saving relationship with Jesus Christ. However, you need not limit the group to believers only. Those who have not yet believed will have several invitations to respond to Christ through repentance and faith. They will have many opportunities to see the contrast between a life that is transformed by Christ and one that is not. This might be their opportunity to encounter the living God and choose to trust Christ.

Order Resources
Each participant will need a Bible study book (item 001303830). Because each person will need to give individual responses to the learning activities, a married couple will need to have two books instead of sharing one copy. You will also need one *Downpour Bible Study Kit* (item 001303831) for your small group. The kit includes one copy of this Bible study book, one copy of the hardcover *Downpour* book, and three DVDs. The DVD sessions have a weekly teaching session from James MacDonald and either a testimony or a worship-music video at the end of each session.

To order resources, write to LifeWay Resources Customer Service; One LifeWay Plaza; Nashville, TN 37234-0113; email orderentry@lifeway.com; fax 615-251-5933; phone toll free 800-458-2772; order online at LifeWay.com; or visit a LifeWay Christian Store.

Secure Equipment and Supplies

Secure the following equipment and supplies for use during the sessions.

- ❑ Television or projector and DVD player
- ❑ Name tags and markers
- ❑ Marker board and markers
- ❑ Extra pens or pencils
- ❑ Roster for keeping attendance records if desired
- ❑ Three-by-five-inch cards for members' contact information

Preview the Course

You may prefer to study the entire Bible study book and view all DVD messages before beginning the study with your small group. However, you may study one week ahead of your group and have a good experience. Before the first session view session 1 on the DVD and study week 1 (pp. 7–20). Be prepared to explain that members will use this book to complete five daily lessons each week and will participate in a weekly small-group session.

Be Ready to Introduce James

Read "About the Author" on page 4 and be prepared to introduce James MacDonald to your group at the first session. To find out more about his ministries, go to:

- www.harvestbible.org
- www.walkintheword.org
- www.lifeway.com/jamesmacdonald

The latter site describes Bible studies by James MacDonald that are offered by Life-Way Christian Resources.

Make Session Plans

The first session is an introductory session with a full, 56-minute video message. Sessions 2–11 can be divided into two relatively equal parts:

Part 1: Discussing the previous week's lesson

Part 2: Viewing and discussing the DVD teaching segment

If you have a 90-minute session, spend the first 30 to 40 minutes in part 1 and use the remainder of the time for part 2. If you have more or less time, adjust the times accordingly. If you have only one hour, use 20 minutes for part 1 and 40 minutes for part 2.

Prepare for Each Session

1. Use the information cards (described in session 1) and pray for the members of your group during the week. Be sensitive to the Holy Spirit's prompting about possibly making a phone call or sending a note of encouragement. As you become aware of members' prayer concerns, jot notes on their cards so that you can pray specifically for their needs.

2. Study the content for the previous week (for example, study week 1 before session 2).

3. Preview the DVD message for the upcoming session.

4. Review the session plans that follow for the upcoming session, together with the activities described on the introductory pages at the beginning of the corresponding week's content material. (For instance, session 1 below corresponds to the introductory pages for week 1, found on pages 8–9.) Determine which activities and questions will be best for use with your group. Decide on a tentative time schedule for the session so that you will have time for each segment of the session.

5. Secure a television or projector, a DVD player, and the DVDs from *Downpour Bible Study Kit*. Make sure they work properly.

6. If members will need them, provide name tags weekly so that they can get better acquainted.

7. Provide a marker board or chart paper and markers for notes, lists, or prayer concerns that may surface during the session.

Session 1
we need a downpour

See the session activities on pages 8–9.

This introductory session will require at least 90 minutes to allow time for the DVD message and small-group interaction.

1. On a marker board or chart paper list information you would like each member to provide you on a three-by-five-inch card so that you can stay in touch with them throughout the study.
2. Greet members as they arrive. Ask them to prepare a name tag and to write the information you desire on a three-by-five-inch card.
3. Record each person's name on a class roster, if desired; distribute books; and collect book fees, if any.
4. Open with prayer for the upcoming study of *Downpour*. Pray for personal revival in the life of every participant.
5. Invite members to turn to page 8. Guide them in the get-acquainted activity.
6. Introduce James MacDonald, using information on page 4.
7. Point members to the DVD message notes and encourage them to fill in the blanks during the DVD message. Mention the time frame (56 min.) for this first introductory message and explain that future messages will be divided into two parts to allow more time for group interaction.
8. Point members to the "Downpour" song lyrics on page 10. Suggest that they follow along as the song is sung at the end of today's message.
9. View session 1 on the DVD and follow the suggestions in "Responding to the Message" on page 9.
10. Explain the use of the workbook and encourage members to complete the study on pages 10–20 prior to your next session.
11. Follow the instructions in "Small-Group Agreements" on page 9.

Session 2
God on the throne: a picture of holiness, part 1

See the session activities on pages 22–23.

Before the Session
❏ Review "Prepare for Each Session" on page 168.
❏ Review the recommended session activities on pages 22–23 and the additional suggestions below. Determine which discussion questions and activities will be most helpful for your group.

During the Session
In addition to the suggestions on pages 22–23, consider the following.
1. Call on a volunteer to recite Hosea 6:1 (this week's key verse to memorize). Encourage members to memorize the key verse each week.
2. Discuss what you learned from Josiah's personal revival on pages 14–15.
3. Examine the high points on your spiritual timeline (p. 17) and discuss ways these times may have been sparked by a crisis in your life as James described last week.
4. What did you learn from Jonathan Edwards's picture of personal revival that might be valuable insights for today (pp. 19–20)?
5. Explain that the remaining DVD messages are divided into two parts. This week's message is the first half of the "God on the Throne" message.
6. Read the snapshot summary and goals for this week (p. 23) and pray for your group prior to viewing the DVD message.
7. How has God impacted your thinking or feelings as you have listened to "Downpour" on the Message-Music CD this week?

Session 3
God on the throne: a picture of holiness, part 2

See the session activities on pages 36–37.

Before the Session
- ❑ Review "Prepare for Each Session" on page 168.
- ❑ Review the recommended session activities on pages 36–37 and the additional suggestions below. Determine which discussion questions and activities will be most helpful for your group.

During the Session
In addition to the suggestions on pages 36–37, consider the following.
1. Call on a volunteer to recite Isaiah 6:3.
2. Discuss what you learned from Hezekiah's personal revival (pp. 33–34).
3. Read the snapshot summary and goals for this week (p. 37) and pray for your group just prior to viewing the DVD message.
4. After the DVD message take time as a group to process the meaning of the message in "The Glory of God" by completing the activities on page 38.

NOTES

....

....

....

....

....

....

Session 4
sin in the mirror: a picture of brokenness, part 1

See the session activities on pages 50–51.

Before the Session
- ❑ Review "Prepare for Each Session" on page 168.
- ❑ Review the recommended session activities on pages 50–51 and the additional suggestions below. Determine which discussion questions and activities will be most helpful for your group.

During the Session
In addition to the suggestions on pages 50–51, consider the following.
1. Call on a volunteer to recite 1 Peter 1:15.
2. How has God impacted your thinking or feelings as you have listened to "The Glory of God" on the Message-Music CD this week?
3. Read the snapshot summary and goals for this week (p. 51) and pray for your group just prior to viewing the DVD message.

NOTES

....

....

....

....

....

....

....

Session 5
sin in the mirror: a picture of brokenness, part 2

See the session activities on pages 64–65.

Before the Session
- ☐ Review "Prepare for Each Session" on page 168.
- ☐ Review the recommended session activities on pages 64–65 and the additional suggestions below. Determine which discussion questions and activities will be most helpful for your group.

During the Session
In addition to the suggestions on pages 64–65, consider the following.
1. Call on a volunteer to recite Romans 1:18.
2. Read the snapshot summary and goals for this week (p. 65) and pray for your group just prior to viewing the DVD message.
3. Discuss what you learned from David's personal revival (pp. 61–62).
4. After the DVD message take time as a group to process the meaning of the message in "Good and Faithful Friend" by completing the activities on page 66.
5. Ask: What are the benefits of hearing the truth from a doctor when you have a serious illness? How does that principle of knowing the truth even when it hurts apply to identifying your sin? Can anyone relate a story about the way a wrong physical diagnosis led to negative consequences? Can anyone relate a story about the way a painfully truthful physical diagnosis led to healing?

NOTES

....

....

Session 6
self in the dirt: a picture of repentance, part 1

See the session activities on pages 78–79.

Before the Session
- ☐ Review "Prepare for Each Session" on page 168.
- ☐ Review the recommended session activities on pages 78–79 and the additional suggestions below. Determine which discussion questions and activities will be most helpful for your group.

During the Session
In addition to the suggestions on pages 78–79, consider the following.
1. Call on a volunteer to recite James 5:16.
2. How has God impacted your thinking or feelings as you have listened to "Good and Faithful Friend" on the Message-Music CD this week?
3. Read the snapshot summary and goals for this week (p. 79) and pray for your group just prior to viewing the DVD message.
4. Discuss what you learned from the picture of personal revival for the Derksen brothers (pp. 75–76).

NOTES

....

....

....

....

....

....

....

Session 7
self in the dirt: a picture of repentance, part 2

See the session activities on pages 92–93.

Before the Session

☐ Review "Prepare for Each Session" on page 168.

☐ Review the recommended session activities on pages 92–93 and the additional suggestions below. Determine which discussion questions and activities will be most helpful for your group.

☐ Consider getting some burlap or other rough cloth. Cut enough pieces the size of a book mark to give one to each person in the group. During the session discuss the significance of sackcloth and the example in the repentance at Nineveh. Encourage members to place the bookmarks in a book or their Bibles for a period as a physical reminder of the need for humility and serious repentance.

During the Session

In addition to the suggestions on pages 92–93, consider the following.
1. Call on a volunteer to recite 1 Corinthians 7:10.
2. Discuss what you learned from Johah's personal revival (pp. 89–90).
3. Read the snapshot summary and goals for this week (p. 93) and pray for your group just prior to viewing the DVD message.
4. After the DVD message take time as a group to process the meaning of the message in "Beautiful God" by completing the activities on page 94.

Session 8
Christ on the cross: a picture of grace, part 1

See the session activities on pages 106–7.

Before the Session

☐ Review "Prepare for Each Session" on page 168.

☐ Review the recommended session activities on pages 106–7 and the additional suggestions below. Determine which discussion questions and activities will be most helpful for your group.

During the Session

In addition to the suggestions on pages 106–7, consider the following.
1. Call on a volunteer to recite Acts 3:19-20.
2. How has God impacted your thinking or feelings as you have listened to "Beautiful God" on the Message-Music CD this week?
3. Discuss what you learned from the picture of personal revival for Evan Roberts and Wales (pp. 103–4).
4. Read the snapshot summary and goals for this week (p. 107) and pray for your group just prior to viewing the DVD message.

NOTES

....

....

....

....

....

....

....

....

Session 9
Christ on the cross: a picture of grace, part 2

See the session activities on pages 120–21.

Before the Session
- ❑ Review "Prepare for Each Session" on page 168.
- ❑ Review the recommended session activities on pages 120–21 and the additional suggestions below. Determine which discussion questions and activities will be most helpful for your group.

During the Session
In addition to the suggestions on pages 120–21, consider the following.
1. Call on a volunteer to recite Galatians 6:14.
2. Read the snapshot summary and goals for this week (p. 121) and pray for your group just prior to viewing the DVD message.
3. After the DVD message take time as a group to process the meaning of the message in "Sea of Grace" by completing the activities on page 122.

NOTES

....

....

....

....

....

....

....

Session 10
Spirit in control: a picture of power, part 1

See the session activities on pages 134–35.

Before the Session
- ❑ Review "Prepare for Each Session" on page 168.
- ❑ Review the recommended session activities on pages 134–35 and the additional suggestions below. Determine which discussion questions and activities will be most helpful for your group.

During the Session
In addition to the suggestions on pages 134–35, consider the following.
1. Call on a volunteer to recite Colossians 1:13-14.
2. Read the snapshot summary and goals for this week (p. 135) and pray for your group just prior to viewing the DVD message.

NOTES

....

....

....

....

....

....

....

....

Session 11
Spirit in control: a picture of power, part 2

See the session activities on pages 148–49.

Before the Session
- ❑ Review "Prepare for Each Session" on page 168.
- ❑ Review the recommended session activities on pages 148–49 and the additional suggestions below. Determine which discussion questions and activities will be most helpful for your group.

During the Session
In addition to the suggestions on pages 148–49, consider the following.
1. Call on a volunteer to recite Ephesians 5:18.
2. Read the snapshot summary and goals for this week (p. 149) and pray for your group just prior to viewing the DVD message.
3. Before watching the DVD message, mention that James will lead a prayer time at the conclusion of His message. Encourage members to join that prayer time and respond to the Lord and not just be spectators.
4. After the DVD message take time as a group to process the meaning of the message in "Come, Let Us Return" by completing the activities on page 150.

NOTES

....

....

....

....

....

Session 12
He will come to us like the rain

See the session activities on pages 162–63.

Before the Session
- ❑ Review "Prepare for Each Session" on page 168.
- ❑ Review the recommended session activities on pages 162–63 and the additional suggestions below. Determine which discussion questions and activities will be most helpful for your group.

During the Session
In addition to the suggestions on pages 162–63, consider the following.
1. Call on a volunteer to recite Romans 8:13.
2. How has God impacted your thinking or feelings as you have listened to "Come, Let Us Return" on the Message-Music CD this week?
3. Discuss with the group options for growth in discipleship following your study of *Downpour*. Visit lifeway.com/jamesmacdonald for options.

NOTES

....

....

....

....

....

....

HARVEST SONGS

For more information about the ministry and music

resources of Harvest Songs or to purchase a full

CD of "Downpour Revival Songs," visit

harvestsongs.org.